BLUE VEINS AND
KINKY HAIR

BLUE VEINS AND KINKY HAIR

Naming and Color Consciousness in African America

Obiagele Lake

PRAEGER

Westport, Connecticut
London

Library of Congress Cataloging-in-Publication Data

Lake, Obiagele.
    Blue veins and kinky hair : naming and color consciousness in African America/
Obiagele Lake.
        p. cm.
    Includes bibliographical references and index.
    ISBN 0–89789–558–4 (alk. paper)
        1. African Americans—Race identity.   2. Names, Personal—African American.
    3. Race awareness—United States.   I.   Title.
    E185.625 L35   2003
    305.896'073—dc21   2002066349

British Library Cataloguing in Publication Data is available.

Library of Congress Catalog Card Number: 2002066349
ISBN: 0–89789–558–4

First published in 2003

Praeger Publishers, 88 Post Road West, Westport, CT 06881
An imprint of Greenwood Publishing Group, Inc.
www.praeger.com

Printed in the United States of America

The paper used in this book complies with the
Permanent Paper Standard issued by the National
Information Standards Organization (Z39.48–1984).

10 9 8 7 6 5 4 3 2 1

Contents

Acknowledgments

I am indebted to many people who have generously supported me through the writing of this manuscript. I want to especially thank the staff at the Charleston (SC) County Library and those at the Avery Research Center for African American History and Culture. Special thanks to Deborah Wright for her support and guidance through the Brown Fellowship Society records.

I also want to express my deep affection and appreciation to my son, Jahmal Lake, and Jane Guinetti, who offered valuable critiques to this manuscript. I also send my deepest gratitude to Brenda Crawford, who gave me moral and material support for my research in South Carolina.

Preface

When Europeans extracted Africans from their homelands, they brought with them a cultural philosophy that legitimated the slaughter and enslavement of millions of African people. While physically and politically dismembering Africans, they also created religious and secular ideologies that, in their minds, rationalized their heinous deeds. These philosophies began with explorers, missionaries, traders, and colonists who viewed their invasions as sanctioned by god. This sense of righteousness was later elaborated by artists, philosophers, and anthropologists who planted the idea of a superior European race.

Chief among these racist ideologues was Joseph Arthur de Gobineau, a French writer and diplomat, who proposed a hierarchy of races—"white, yellow, and black." According to him, only the "Aryan ["White"] race," possessed superior intellectual, physical, and cultural attributes. In his *Essai sur L'inegalite des Races Humaines, 1835–1855* (The Inequality of the Races, 1835–1855), he warned that the downfall of any civilization would result from miscegenation among various racial groups. Gobineau was followed by a number of European theorists who advocated the purity of German Aryans and the inferiority of all other peoples, placing African people at the bottom of the racial hierarchy.[1]

Secular philosophies from all corners of the European world deemed Africans mentally and physically inferior to European people (Harris 1968: 80–107). Avid proponents of these theories included Scottish anatomist Robert Knox (*The Races of Men*, 1850) and European Americans J.C. Nott and G.R. Gliddon (*Types of Mankind*, 1854). A number of other scientists of the period, anthropologists among them, added to the mix of racist evolutionary typology.

Religious ideology joined these secular attacks to act as a fifth column in disparaging African people.

Europeans interpreted Christian religious texts in a way that would crystallize their campaign of cultural and racial hegemony. The story of Ham is but one example. Ham, the son of Noah, fearing rivalry from a sibling, objected to his father having another child. When his father did not relent, Ham castrated him. As a result, Ham and his offspring (the Canaanites) were summarily cursed with black skin. Europeans (and European Americans) equated the cursed black skin of Ham and the black skin of Africans, which allowed them to justify their exploitation of African people by sacralizing racist doctrines.

Beginning in the eighteenth century, European and European American physicians and social scientists more fully developed racial determinist theories. In an attempt to answer questions regarding the various states of human development among different races, many proposed that African and European people belonged to two separate species. According to polygenists, the European (or Caucasian) was presumed to be the original prototype against which all other "human species" should be measured. According to Marvin Harris (1971:86), Reverend Samuel Smith (the seventh president of Princeton College) averred that Africans' dark pigmentation "was nothing more than a huge freckle that covered the whole body as a result of an oversupply of bile." Racial determinism was also touted by revered eighteenth- and nineteenth-century European philosophers, such as David Hume and Voltaire (François-Marie Arouet). Hume wrote:

There never was a civilized nation of any other complexion than white, nor even any individual eminent either in act or speculation. No ingenious manufacturer among them, no arts, no sciences.... Such a uniform and constant difference could not happen, in so many countries and ages, if nature had not made an original distinction betwixt these breeds of men. (quoted in Curtin 1964:42)

From the French quarter, Voltaire, who is known for his attacks on inequality and injustice, wrote:

If their [Africans'] understanding is not of a different nature from ours, it is at least greatly inferior. They are not capable of any great application or association of ideas, and seemed formed neither for the advantages nor the abuses of philosophy. (quoted in Gossett 1963:45)

Hume and Voltaire are but two luminaries and European racists whose ideas were incorporated into European American ideology that posited Africans closer to animals than human beings. Many of these ideas were popular within the "American School," one of the first formal schools of anthropological thought in the United States, which was founded Samuel Morton, a Philadelphia physician. Morton measured Caucasian, African, and Asian skulls and argued that divine intervention had created different human species. Morton's disciples, George Giddon and Josiah Nott, elaborated on his work and in *Types of Mankind* asserted that "the races of man were separately created species, and that each possessed a 'constant and undeviating' physical and moral nature which could be changed only by interbreeding" (cited in M. Harris 1971:91). The proliferation of these dogma and other racist ideologies operated to justify theories of "Manifest Destiny" in the Americas and "The White Man's Burden" in Africa.

Moreover, these theories were widely disseminated and embraced by the common populace because it gave them moral solace while exacting savagery against African people (and at the same time Native Americans). Well after the end of slavery, invasions into Africa for the usurpation of land and the extraction of free labor persisted.

On the other side of the Atlantic, Jim Crow laws replicated uneven relations between African and European Americans extant during slavery. Reconstruction amendments gave African Americans *de jure* freedom when, in fact, elite European Americans ruled the day and African Americans had no rights that any European American needed to respect. Consequently, Africans in America remained disenfranchised and dehumanized. Not only did they not enjoy citizenship rights in a land that they had built, but they were led to believe that they were not worthy of these rights based on their African ancestry. When Europeans first exploited Africans in the fourteenth century, they instilled the idea that Africans were without intelligence, without culture, and without beauty.

The African body was deemed grotesque and bestial. The idea that the African body was grotesque and less than human was not only given credence by the vast majority of Europeans but Africans themselves absorbed the idea that they were less than beautiful. Europeans suggested that Africans' dark skin, kinky hair, flat noses, and full lips were ugly. In addition to these ideological and symbolic lacerations of the African body, Europeans replaced African names with European varieties and, thus, rounded off the physical rape of Africa and its people. The resulting emotional and psychic damage contributed to the killing of individual and collective self-worth.

The devaluation and, indeed, in some cases, the elimination of names and the denigration of body characteristics and somatotypes represents a cultural loss that rivals political-economic marginalization. The purpose of this book is to delineate how Africans in America internalized the negative images created by the European world. This internalized racism has worked to fracture African American unity and thereby dilute inchoate efforts toward liberation. This has worked well for members of the dominant society who realize that once they convince people of African descent that their very persons are repulsive they have won the ultimate battle. Psychological warfare was the coup de grâce that has reverberated throughout generations and has mollified and confused African people.

As Fanon (1968:210–211) adeptly points out:

When we consider the efforts made to carry out the cultural estrangement so characteristic of the colonial epoch, we realize that nothing has been left to chance and that the total result looked for by colonial domination was indeed to convince the native that colonialism came to lighten their darkness. The effect consciously sought by colonialism was to drive into the natives' heads the idea that if the settlers were to leave, they would at once fall back into barbarism, degradation, and bestiality.

   Indeed, the process of colonizing Africa and scattering its citizens into a "new world," of necessity, included a redefinition of people and land so that it would seem that the colonized had had no identity of their own. At the same time, nominally transforming people into colors and assigning them a nonhuman status allowed European savage behaviors to seem humane since they were convinced of the correctness of their deeds. The real tragedy in this centuries-long drama is that Africans themselves came to incorporate and accept their new names and the grotesque images molded by European and European American hands. While Africans in America maintained their cultural practices and beliefs, at the same time, a large segment of the population suffered from cultural and psychological damage as a result of internalizing racist ideologies. Only recently, in the past few decades, have writers chosen to grapple with the ramifications of internalized racism and how this is manifested in bodily control.

   The internalization of stereotypes has compelled a large sector of diaspora Africans (and continental Africans to a lesser degree) to reject their own image and attempt to replicate European standards. This process has been manifested by de-kinking African hair and adulating light skin. This is significant because in order for any people to succeed they must first know and love who they are. Since African Americans have a diluted sense of who they are culturally and racially, it follows that their struggle (if they are struggling at all) is one for individual gain and not for self-determination as a people.

   Instead of developing ideologies that center on cultural and economic solidarity, the majority of African Americans have focused on individual gain. The problem with this approach is that it maintains an uneven, multi-tiered society where those with few resources continue to be oppressed. Almost all African American leaders have failed to grasp this point. The exceptions were not broad-based enough to make a significant difference in affecting the masses of people.

   The Black Power and the pan-African movements in the 1960s possessed the nucleus that might have produced a cultural awareness that could have engendered the collective strength sorely needed in this community. Their failure to do this was due, in part, to the diffusion of human rights strategies within the African American community and the fact that most participants in these movements had also absorbed the values of European American capitalist society. Even groups that appeared to be radical did not actually promote revolutionary ideas or actions.

   In addition to establishing free breakfast programs and community schools, the Black Panthers advocated a community-centered socialist platform, at least theoretically. Their movement was crushed as a result of police tyranny, unrealistic political ideals, disunity, and drug use among the leadership. From a cultural perspective, they understood the relationship between body image and political ideals. All Panthers wore naturals and promoted African hair as a symbol that represented self-love and racial unity. Although they, along with other activists discussed in Chapter 4, encouraged many African Americans to "go natural," unfortunately, most African Americans had already learned that "nappy was not nice" and continued to process their hair. Moreover, the Panthers themselves wore their 'fros only superficially since they ridiculed pan-Africanist ideologies of the time and were constantly at odds with African Americans who espoused these theories. In addition, many people considered the Panthers' political stance "too militant"—they carried guns and dared the police to exact brutality in their communities.

Kwame Ture (aka Stokely Carmichael), one of the most prominent pan-Africanist leaders in the United States, also emphasized self-love and the importance of embracing one's African identity, which included loving our hair, dark skin, broad noses, and full lips. He also understood the importance of names and insisted that "We Are Africans." Ture's All African People's Revolutionary Party (AAPRP) organized cells at various universities across the country and caught the attention of a small sector of students who were taught the ostensible sanctity of Kwame Nkrumah's scientific socialism. Not only had most of these students never heard of Nkrumah (the first president of Ghana), but the AAPRP's political message ran counter to the capitalist mind frame into which their ephemeral constituency was born. Nevertheless, Black Power and pan-African movements had sufficiently influenced a segment of African Americans who did not straighten their hair or shed their African names when the 1960s ended. Despite this, the vast majority continued the centuries-old practice of attempting to assimilate into European American society.

Chapter 1 attempts to show how group and personal names, including racial epithets, have had far-reaching and deep-seated effects on African American self-perceptions. Even though the ephitet "Black" is considered a milestone by many African Americans, a color name, an adjective, extracts African Americans from the realm of human society and cultural existence and deposits them into the realm of inanimate objects. A color name, especially in the midst of an environment replete with stereotypes that degrade its referent, adds credence to the myth of inferiority. Throughout history this inferior image has been exacerbated by mixed-race people—many of whom repudiated their African roots in favor of their European heritage.

Chapter 2 discusses the rape of African women on slave ships and plantations, which gave rise to a mulatto population of noticeable proportions. European men who fathered these children often conferred economic privilege on their mixed offspring—a factor that economically put many mulattoes a step above their darker kin. Mulattoes held themselves aloof from the larger African American population and, in many cases, built exclusive institutions that admitted only members from within the mulatto upper class. If they were light enough to "pass," they sought to marry even lighter or "white" partners until any hint of African ancestry was erased. Despite the ubiquitousness and longevity of these practices, some scholars try to argue that colorism among African Americans was and is insignificant. In actuality, colorism, along with classism, was a primary factor that determined the nature of intraracial and interracial relations.

Organizations such as the Brown Fellowship Society and the Blue Vein Society, among others, distanced themselves from the larger African American community and based their membership on skin color, hair texture, and economic status. Thus, a wealthy dark-skinned person would have been ineligible for membership in these societies, as would a light-skinned person of insufficient means. But all else being equal, eligibility was grounded on skin color and hair texture. Not only did mulattoes see themselves as superior based on their European characteristics but so did darker skinned African Americans.

The development of technology facilitated African American attempts to transform their African features, especially their hair, to more closely approximate that of Europeans. African American women, who bore the stigma of lasciviousness and promiscuity, especially desired to shed their African skins and process their kinky hair in an attempt to perfect the Victorian model: upright, cultured, and pure. In Chapter 3, I discuss the role of hair culturists who, beginning in the late nineteenth century, contributed to this charade. Annie Turnbo and Sarah Walker (Madam C. J. Walker) became millionaires by producing and marketing cosmetics and establishing hairdressing schools in the United States and abroad. A number of Europeans and other African Americans joined the bandwagon in search of fortunes by marketing the transformation of African American hair and skin color. While most African Americans promoted the "White" ideal, in the 1960s, the Black Power and the pan-African movements in the African Diaspora and independence struggles in Africa were two primary factors that precipitated the need for recollecting African roots.

Even though the cultural aspects of the Black Power and the pan-African movements of the 1960s and 1970s had long-lasting effects on a small sector of the African American population, the vast majority remain mired in a sea of exotic images that promise to make them more acceptable to the majority population. Not surprisingly, most people who straighten their hair do not concede that this practice is a manifestation of self-hate, claiming instead that processed hair is simply a matter of style. In Chapter 4, I address these arguments by pointing to verbal assaults on African Americans, especially females, who have chosen to accentuate their kinky hair. Moreover, a medley of African American limericks that ridicule dark skin and kinky hair have persisted throughout the centuries. This chapter clearly delineates ways in which European Americans also favor processed hair and light skin. To cite but one example, women with natural hair, whether they wear short-cropped Afros, braids, or dreadlocks, have been fired or threatened with dismissal if they did not "change" their hair.

African American repudiation of racial and cultural heritage has coincided with political–economic strategies that have blended into racist and classist European American ideologies. While many assimilationist African Americans have moved into the middle class, one-third of the population remains below the poverty line. Unfortunately, those at the bottom of the barrel have also changed their physical images in the hope of mimicking those who have "succeeded." While it is true that we have won many battles in the struggle for progress and inclusion, we have yet to gain liberation for the masses of African people because we remain splintered in terms of who we are. A unitary definition and representation as people of African descent would channel our strategies and replace the diluted versions that have characterized African American movements up until now. In a phrase, the lack of political solidarity in the United States and in the African Diaspora on the whole is coterminous with the absence of an African cultural identity that would unite us.

This analysis is significant because it points to the connection between identity and political solidarity—an area of research that has only recently been explored. The underlying problem is that Africans in the Americas have divorced themselves from themselves. While this is not the case for all people of African descent, feelings of inferiority have been normal enough to preclude a united protracted struggle that would radically change their political and economic status.

NOTE

1. Gobineau's most influential admirers included composer Richard Wagner, who extolled the virtues of Nordic Germans in his musical productions. Houston Stewart Chamberlain, an Englishman who adopted German nationality, linked himself with Gobineau and Wagner in his book *Die Grundlagen des 19. Jahrhunderts* (The Foundations of the Nineteenth Century, 1899). While all of these racists considered Africans to be inferior in every way, they also targeted Jews as the spoilers of Jesus' doctrine and advocated the suppression of Judaism. Like his cohorts, Chamberlain believed that Jews poisoned the "Aryan doctrine." His solution was to eliminate them along with Judaism.

Chapter 1

Renaming African People

The power of nomination is absolute power. Given the Europeans' penchant to usurp land and human beings, the ability to rename African people was the coup de grâce that ratified and, in their minds, justified the plunder of a continent and its people. Similar to their disparagement of African hair and skin color, Europeans bestowed individual and group names on African people that designated their capture and their inferior position in society.

Europeans wielded these new identities in order to convince Africans of the rightness of their subjugation and to further estrange them from their culture, land, language, and history. Before the arrival of Europeans in Africa, Africans referred to themselves by many different terms that represented their cultural and geopolitical statuses. As they had in other conquered territories, Europeans ignored the values held by these cultures and renamed African people to accommodate their own needs and their own perceptions.

The renaming of African people is significant because cultural identities embody people's values. Assigned names had no corollaries in African societies, thus, these nomenclatures operated, and continue to operate, to alienate African people from themselves. From the perspective of European colonizers, the ostensible necessity for changing names falls within the process of what Ali Mazrui (1986) calls the "dis-Africanisation" of diaspora Africans.

The slave condition was in this sense a case of engineered or contrived amnesia. In most cases, the idea was to reduce the risk of nostalgia and the desire to escape. So much of the history of the slave experience in the Western hemisphere amounted to the following command addressed to the captives. Forget you are African, remember you are black! Forget you are African, remember you are black! (109–113)

Not only were Africans defined in terms of color, but the European process of devaluing other aspects of African culture—for example, family structures, religion, and art—combined to make Africans in the Americas "ashamed of their place of origin. The destruction of the Afro-American capacity for cultural nostalgia was complete in the bulk of the population" (112).

Throughout the centuries, a large proportion of people of African descent in the Western Hemisphere have attempted to divorce themselves from their African origins (Skinner and Robinson 1983) and, in the process, have accepted labels that are ahistorical and acultural. The extent of this dis-Africanization was epitomized by William Ferris (1913:296) when he wrote: "After the Negrosaxon has been made over into the likeness of the white man he can hope to be made over into the image of God[!]." Even though these words were written at the beginning of the twentieth century, many African Americans continue to adulate European cultural symbols at the expense of their own.

While there is an enormous amount of material that focuses on the political-economic aspects of slavery (see, for example, Conniff 1994; Franklin 1994; Kolchin 1993) and racism (Hacker 1992; Marable 1991; Pinkney 1984), not enough attention has been given to the psychological and cultural repercussions of slavery and its aftermath. This chapter emphasizes the connection between identity and language and calls attention to the "interlocking process of self-identification and self-determination" (Wilkinson 1990:15). Moreover, the examination of names and naming draws attention to the fact that language not only gives us a medium to express our thoughts but also influences what we are capable of thinking.

A nomenclature that is not historically contextualized lays the groundwork in which individual interests thrive and collective consciousness has no meaning. This is an important point because solidarity is the key to African American progress. I further propose that the obstacles that prevent African Americans from organizing toward a united front against racism are the very same ones that preclude their ability to agree on a common name that is representative of their cultural history. These barriers include the fact that African Americans, like other diaspora Africans, have been historically conditioned to uphold the individualistic and materialistic values of capitalism—values that inherently work against the advancement of the masses of African American people and other historically oppressed peoples (Blauner 1972:146–148). That African Americans have internalized negative self-images (Du Bois 1920:263, 266; 1933:199–200; Mazrui 1986:109–113) is also a major factor that works in tandem with individualistic goals and precludes consolidation with other diaspora and continental Africans. Failure to recognize this is due, in part, to the ubiquitousnous of negative images imposed on African Americans—a factor that motivates their haste to escape these representations and one that normalizes their stigmatization.

Attention to the significance of naming is not foreign to anthropologists who have addressed this issue as it pertains to other societies, some of which are diaspora African (Azevedo 1980:360–363; Carcucci 1984:143–155; Chuks-Orji 1972; Lasker 1980:525–538). Absent in the field of anthropology is a close study of names that apply to African Americans and how naming, as a linguistic device, is intricately tied to identity issues (see Katz and Braly 1935–1936; Williams, Tucker, and Dunham 1971:222–228).

Anthropologists are also active participants in the arena of identity politics (for example, Dominguez 1994; Safran 1991:89–90; Scott 1992:12–19), yet the identity of African Americans is either misrepresented or completely factored out of this discourse. This dimunization of African American identity is facilitated by anthropologists who propose that "race" does not exist, that it is merely a social construction.

The "logic" behind their reasoning is embodied in the proposal that all human beings share the same genes. In terms of African Americans, and other groups who are defined as distinctive racial groups, anthropologists claim that they have more genes in common with European Americans than they share within their own group.

While it may satisfy anthropologists to claim that race is a noncategory— and it may even soothe the racism that gave birth to their discipline—it does not change the fact that Africans are a distinctive people both culturally and phenotypically. The latter is especially important because our physical distinctiveness, the ability of European Americans to easily identify us, is what enables them to continue institutionalizing barriers that impede our progress, and this while they write the words that race is a phantom category.

Regardless of anthropological theories, African Americans, as a whole, view themselves as a distinctive racial and cultural group. Although many have internalized stereotypical characterizations, at the same time, they do not equate the *concept* of race with inferiority until it is suggested that they do so. Thinking of different racial groups as inferior has been a very European phenomenon.

The fact that we are easily identifiable was in part responsible for our capture and subsequent brutalization in America and beyond. So, while race may not be *solely* biological, biology has played a large role in our unique experience in slavery and its legacy. I suspect that many anthropologists, as well as others, assume that eliminating the *idea* of race is tantamount to erasing the institution of racism. Oh, that it could be so simple.

Concomitant with this attempt to symbolically erase the idea of race are efforts to debunk strategies for race-based political mobilization. Anthropologists and other social scientists brandish such words as red herrings, convincing *others* that essentializing and totalizing is unsophisticated, implying that the struggle for rights must be a humane endeavor devoid of racial connotations. Denise Riley's (1988) attempt to recast Sojourner Truth's memorable statement in 1851 is indicative of twentieth century European American cultural (and academic) hegemony.

Riley suggests that instead of asking a group of European American men "Ain't I a woman?,"[1] Truth *should* have asked "Ain't I a fluctuating identity?" (emphasis in Riley's original). In one phrase, Riley presumes to redefine African Americans' and the womanist perspective embodied in Truth's testimony. If Riley had respected Truth's right to identify herself based on her own experience, she would have understood that surviving and being recognized as a freedom fighter were far more important than "fluctuating" her identity. The significance of Truth's explanation of her name is embodied in her own words:

I go round a' testifyin' and showin' their signs agin my people. My name was Isabella [Baumfree], but when I left the house of bondage, I left everything behind. ... I went to the Lord and asked him to give me a new name, and the Lord gave me Sojourner because I was to travel up an' down the land, showin' people their sins.... Afterward I told the Lord I wanted another name...and the Lord gave me Truth. (quoted in Sterling 1984:151)

Riley unwittingly raises the fundamental question of whose definitions count. Because the emic view has ostensibly been a sought-after and respected perspective in anthropology, it would follow that the emic view among African Americans should carry more weight than anthropological theories about who African Americans are. Other groups in the United States have more easily created their own identities, given their privileged position in society.

Nineteenth- and twentieth-century European immigrants were once divided on the basis of nationality and culture. Some groups, like the Irish and Southern Italians, were considered separate races and were discriminated against (although not to the same systematic degree as people of African descent). The ability of these marginalized groups to blend into Anglo-American society was based on their racial similarity with other Europeans, as well as opportunities to adopt Anglo-American cultural norms and language. And, although European Americans have held onto aspects of their respective identities, they have tended to line up on the same side against people of African descent (Alba 1990:316–319).

By embracing the "White" nomenclature, European Americans have been able to amalgamate along racial lines, in spite of the genetic heterogeneity among them. Even though the term "White" also homogenizes and is acultural and ahistorical, connotations of this term are replete with positive insinuations compared with "Black," which connotes sinister and deadly deeds (Fairchild 1985; Jordan 1968; Longshore 1979:183–197).

The act of linguistically homogenizing African and European cultures has served to advantage the latter and to deculturalize the former. While most people of European descent in the United States consider themselves to be "White," they also value their European heritage. Given that Africans were torn from their motherland and enslaved in America, it is impossible for most of us to point to our specific points of origin—but we can point to Africa. It is this place of origin that many European Americans would have us forget. As Fanon (1968:41) points out:

It is not enough for the settler to delimit physically....As if to show the totalitarian character of colonial exploitation the settler paints the native as a sort of quintessence of evil. The native is declared insensible to ethics; he represents not only the absence of values, but also the negation of values. . . . He is the corrosive element, destroying all that comes near him; he is the deforming element, disfiguring all that has to do with beauty or morality.

Africans came to believe these characterizations and replaced their own values and myths with those of the colonizer. As Europeans scattered Africans throughout the diaspora, they continued to debauch their cultural systems.

RENAMING OTHER COLONIZED PEOPLES

European racial hegemony created a caste system among African-descended people in Latin America and the Caribbean. Jamaica serves as a good example of this dynamic because it has one of the largest populations of African-descended people in the Antilles and it is the island with which North Americans are most familiar.

The image of Jamaica, created on TV commercials and in travel brochures, is one of a tropical paradise, where beautiful light-skinned women perpetually emerge from sky blue waters and old bearded men tell stories to children under the shade of mango trees. In reality, Jamaica is a neo-colonial outpost where descendants of African slaves continue to struggle without land and without control over their own means of production. This situation evolved from centuries of slavery in which Englishmen exploited Africans for the production of sugar and indigo. As in the United States, the European rape of African women was an integral part of Jamaican slave society and gave rise to a mulatto class that served as a buffer between Europeans and Africans. As Hall (1991) states:

To be colored was to belong to the "mixed" ranks of the brown middle class, a cut above the rest—in aspiration if not in reality. . . . The Caribbean system was organized through the finely graded classification system of the colonial discourses of race, arranged on an ascending scale up to the ultimate "white" term—the latter always out of reach, the impossible, "absent" term, whose absent–presence structures the whole chain. In the bitter struggle for place and position which characterizes dependent societies, every notch on the scale mattered profoundly. The English system, by contrast, was organized around a simple binary dichotomy, more appropriate to the colonizing order. (106–107)

In present-day Jamaica, color remains integral to class (Waters 1985:29–39). The majority of working-class people are darker skinned and the majority of those who make up the elite are "White" or mulatto. According to Nettleford (1973):

Poverty, destitution, and loss of hope is somehow linked with the fact that [African Jamaicans] are of a certain ethnic origin in a country controlled by people of another ethnic origin who think themselves superior. (55)

The degradation of the African image is repeated in the cultural milieu where African (kinky) hair is referred to as "bad hair" and European (straight or curly) is referred to as "good hair" (49). The divisions among Jamaican people are exacerbated by the use of "Black" for dark-skinned people, "brown" for people of mixed African and European heritage, and "red" for still lighter-skinned Jamaicans.

On other Caribbean islands, the myriad terms used to describe people of African descent underscores the meticulous attention paid to color (along with hair texture) and the relative lack of importance placed on national or ancestral origins. In Puerto Rico, for example, there are several terms to describe people with different degrees of African heritage (Fitzpatrick 1971). Even though Puerto Ricans and other Caribbean and Latin American people assert that there is scant preoccupation with color in their societies, the names applied to people based on color and hair texture and the development of these names over the centuries suggest that these assertions require further investigation.

The issue of naming in these regions is complicated as a result of miscegenation, which produced people with varying degrees of African features. *De couleur* is often used to refer to a person of African descent and is further conjugated into other terms including *pardo, moreno, mulatto,* and *trigueno* (see Appendix A for an extended list of color names). *Trigueno*, a Spanish word meaning "the color of wheat," is applied to someone who has brown skin, but European features. A person with light or white skin and kinky hair is called *grifo*. Most people in Puerto Rico, as in the rest of the Western Hemisphere, place a high premium on lighter features and Caucasian hair, as is indicated by the term *pelo male (bad hair)* to indicate a person with African or kinky hair (Fitzpatrick 1971:102). Although people meticulously choose names to designate skin color and hair texture, they tend to lump these differences together when they use national or cultural names.

The battle within Latino (or Hispanic) communities is a case in point. The term "Hispanic" is controversial within this community, some of whom would prefer the term Latino or Hispanic American. Although an umbrella term to describe Hispanic people might be useful in engendering political solidarity, a single identifier would also obfuscate racial differences that exist among these groups. The increase in intermarriage among Hispanics and European Americans is another important factor that makes a single term untenable because many people with Spanish surnames are not Spanish speaking, nor are they Hispanic. This becomes important when set-aside programs are targeted toward Hispanics who are not minorities.

Chicanos, one of the poorest Hispanic minority populations, have chosen a nomenclature that represents their racial and historical experience. It also embodies the outcome of a Native American struggle with European interlopers who annexed their territory and made it a part of the United States (Webster 1992:118–119). Mirande (1985), who sees the term "Black" as the most radical term for African Americans, points to the political and symbolic meaning of the term "Chicano" when she writes:

The pervasive use of "Mexican-American" fails to recognize that "chicanos" is a word self-consciously selected by many persons as a symbolic positive identification with a unique cultural heritage. Many have not realized that Mexican Americans is analogous to Negro, or colored, whereas Chicano is analogous to [B]lack. (1985:2–3)

One of the problems with terms used by Spanish-speaking people is that it lumps together people who do not share cultural or racial backgrounds. For example, there are a number of Native Americans who are Spanish speaking and whose heritage is masked by the terms "Hispanic" or "Latino" (Cortes 1980). Moreover, racial typographies among "Hispanics" range from those who are essentially of European descent to those who are of African descent. That the census indicates that "Hispanics" may include people of any race is evidence of an awareness of this conundrum. While census data do not correlate class with color, in actuality class is positively correlated with skin color—with the most well-off being totally or predominantly of European descent, a fact that adds to racial and economic disparities within the group.

Since the colonization of what has come to be known as America, Europeans have also stripped Native Americans of their original names, just as they stripped them of their land. Native Americans were not Native Americans before Europeans came. They, like Africans, belonged to a number of different cultural groups whose names and totems distinguished them from others (Billard 1974:23; Lockhart 1992). Europeans, and later European Americans, changed these names for their own convenience. In addition to altering group names, personal names were also replaced with European varieties (DeMallie and Ortiz 1994:286; Littlefield and Underhill 1971:33–45; Lockhart 1992; Prucha 1984:673–676).

One Native American who attended boarding school in the 1960s vividly recalled the experience of being renamed:

When we entered the mission school...we encountered a rule that prohibited the use of our language, which was rigidly enforced with a hickory rod, so that the newcomer ... was obliged to go about like a little dummy until he learned to express himself in English. All the boys in our school were given English names, because their Indian names were difficult for the teachers to pronounce. Besides, the aboriginal names were considered by the missionaries as heathenish...And so, in the place of Tae-noo-ga-w-zhe came Philip Sheridan, and that of Wa-Pah,dae, Ulysses S. Grant. (Billard 1974:360)

In the past few decades Native American reparations struggles have been accompanied by court actions to change European contrived names to Native American representations (DeMallie and Ortiz 1994:286). Although at first glance names may seem insignificant in the struggle for self-determination

The degree to which one rejects a given categorization correlates rather precisely to the kind and depth of challenge and resistance one is likely to offer, and correspondingly, the probability that one will be able to force changes in external perceptions and the circumstances that derive from them. (Churchill 1994:292)

African Americans have become so accustomed to the cultural metamorpho-sis that many consider their Europeanized group and personal names as in-nocuous. In fact, their acceptance of these names is concomitant with their acceptance of European standards of beauty—both of which compromise their personal and cultural integrity. The ability of the dominant group to impose these standards and make them stick is indicative of how everyday language is integral to the process of power.

A SOCIAL HISTORY OF AFRICAN AMERICAN NAMES

In an effort to symbolically shed their African origins, similar to the process of blanquemiento (or whitening) among Ecuadorian groups studied by Stutz-man (1981:49), people of African descent have participated in a number of be-haviors to subordinate their ancestral characteristics. These range from straightening hair (Caldwell 1995:267–279; Llorens 1967:139–144), lightening their skin (Hall 1995), and eschewing speech patterns that might be identified as typically "Black," among other behaviors.

Foreign names are so ingrained in our culture that most African Americans do not give them a second thought. Even individuals at the forefront of civil rights movements have failed to see the importance of names as symbols of our history and culture (Rogers 1926:237–238, 255). In the first half of the twenti-eth century, W. E. B. Du Bois' response to a letter from a teenager is a classic example of this:

If a thing is despised, you will not alter matters by changing its name. If men despise Negroes, they will not despise them less if Negroes are called "colored" or "Afro-Americans." (1928:96–97)

Du Bois missed the point. The purpose of giving salience to a representative name for African Americans is not to render them less despicable to European Americans. The importance of an appropriate terminology has more to do with individual integrity, group cohesion and collective consciousness than it does the impression it may or may not have on European Americans. Moreover, even though names in and of themselves may not dismantle political-economic barriers to equal opportunities,

Research in racial and ethnic attitudes has well documented the fact that one's attitude toward a particular racial group is, in part, a function of the racial or ethnic labels asso-ciated with that group. (Fairchild 1985:48)

This conclusion emanates from a survey conducted among European Ameri-can university student volunteers who participated in a study titled "Attitudes About Self and Other" (Fairchild 1985). Researchers presented a list of names—"Negroes," "Blacks," and "Afro-Americans"—and asked students to assign characteristics to each category (see Appendix B). The results show that the term "Afro-Americans" is more often associated with positive traits, compared to the terms "Blacks" or "Negroes." While the effects of labeling on European Americans is not the focus of this book, Fairchild's study sheds some light on the impact of names in shaping attitudes.

A CHRONOLOGY OF NAMES

Jesse Jackson called attention to the cultural significance of the term African American in 1989 (Wilkerson 1989:1, 14), but this was by no means the first call for a representative name for people of African descent in America. Beginning in the slave era and throughout the centuries, there has been a list of names used to refer to African Americans (see Appendix C). Some of the more commonly used names for people of African descent have included "Negro," "colored," "Black," "Afro- and African-American," and "African" (Bowen 1906:30–36; Fortune 1906:194–198; Moses 1978:214–217; Walker 1977:74–76).

In the eighteenth and nineteenth centuries the term African, or some derivative thereof, was used more frequently than it is today. The terms figured prominently in the names of secular and religious organizations. An adumbrated list of these organizations include the African Lodge of Masons (1787), the African Baptist Church (1779), the Free African Society (1787), the Afric-American Female Intelligence Society (1832), the Afro-American League (1887), among others (see Appendix D). These organizations are now defunct or have changed their names. The African Methodist Episcopal Zion Church, popularly known as the AME Zion Church, founded by Richard Allen in 1795 (Miller 1975:14), is one of the few organizations to maintain the name "African" in its title.

Nineteenth-century proponents of the term "Afro-American" were explicit in expressing the importance of a name that reflected a cultural heritage and not a color:

In 1896 J.C. Embry called for the universal adoption of "Afro-American"—for the reason that it was euphonious, beautiful, true...descendants of our African forefathers should neither adopt nor recognize the intended stigma which European and American slave holders invented for us ... and if any man ask you why so, tell him she (Africa) is the land of our origin; and since she is, by the fact of history and ideology, mother of the oldest civilization, the oldest science, the oldest art, she is by eminent fitness placed first in the compound title, "Afro-American." (as quoted in Berry and Blassingame 1982:390)

Many African Americans who campaigned for repatriation to Africa felt a close kinship to continental Africans. Alexander Crummel, one of the foremost advocates of African American emigration, defined himself and others as "African" and often spoke of "[w]e children of Africa in this land" (Rigsby 1987:52). But use of this term did not become widespread due to the emergence of the American Colonization Society (ACS) (1816) and other emigrationist groups. In the first quarter of the nineteenth century, the ACS, followed by other repatriation groups, waged a vigorous campaign to ship Africans back to Africa. These repatriation efforts accelerated the deletion of the word "African" from the names of organizations so that they would not be associated with back-to-Africa movements. In 1835, African Americans attending the National Negro Convention voted to eliminate the term "African" from their organization (7). As emigration movements to Africa expanded (Miller 1975; Redkey 1969; Shick 1980; Uya 1971) other groups followed suit.

During the post-reconstruction period, there was a resurgence of the African theme, along with the term "Afro-American" (Toll 1979:140). In 1899 the National Afro-American League was formed, and in 1892, the *Afro-American* newspaper was established. However, the term "Negro" and "colored" persisted, as is witnessed by the formation of the American Negro Academy (1897) and the National Association for the Advancement of Colored People (1909).

"NEGRO" AND "BLACK"

Early in the history of colonization, the term "negro," written with a small "n," became the nomenclature bestowed on Africans in America (Bennett, 1967; Du Bois 1916; Moore 1960). Other names given to us by people of European descent include "moors," "nigras," "niggers," and so on (Berry and Blassingame 1982:391–392; Isaacs, 1964).

In 1829 David Walker, an African American activist and scholar wrote:

White Americans have applied this term [Negro] to Africans by way of reproach for our color, to aggravate and heighten our miseries, because they have their feet on our throats. (quoted in Berry and Blassingame 1982:392)

In spite of such objections, the term "Negro" was the term of choice up until the first half of the twentieth century (Du Bois 1920, 1933; Williams 1969:18). It is also important to point out that beginning after the Civil War, many African Americans began to protest the use of the term "negro" with a small "n." But it was only in the twentieth century when the Associated Press and the *New York Times* decided to capitalize "Negro" (Isaacs 1964:64) that this usage became accepted by the wider society.

However, the movement from "negro" to "Negro" was a pyrrhic victory, given that we only moved from being a lower-case to an upper-case adjective—and still, in many instances, with a minuscule notation.

In the mid-1960s African Americans used "Black" with pride, a term that just a few decades earlier was considered an insult. Terms such as "Black is Beautiful," (Dansby 1978:71) and "I'm Black and I'm proud" are indicative of its new connotation. Even though many African Americans consider the term to be progressive, in fact it is only an English translation of the Spanish and

Portuguese term "negro" and begs the need for a terminology that would define African-descended people in cultural and historical terms.

The Black Power movement also popularized "Black" and contributed significantly to Black consciousness raising (Lessing and Zagorin 1972; Longshore 1979). "Negro"—even with a capital N, like colored, was still used, but had lost its currency by then and was considered derogatory by most African Americans.

"Negro" was employed as a term of opprobrium interchangeable with "Uncle Tom." Invidious semantic distinctions were made between "Negroes" unable or unwilling to divest themselves of the old slave mentality and "blacks" or Afro-Americans proud of their African past and of being black.

USE OF THE TERM COLORED

The use of the term "colored" was coined by mixed-race people (Ottley 1968:95). In the eighteenth century this population and their descendants created their own caste system, which was marked by color and class. In one case in South Carolina, mixed-race people formed the Brown Fellowship Society, an exclusive mulatto organization that I will discuss in more detail in Chapter 2. Mixed descendants of French and Spanish settlers in New Orleans also distinguished themselves by adopting the terms *gens de couleur* or people of color. This term carried with it all the connotations of higher caste associated with nonblackness and mixed ancestry. In the first half of the nineteenth century, "colored" also became the term of polite usage among free Negroes in the North.

Objections to the term "colored" were duly noted in the African American press. In the September 24, 1831, edition of *The Liberator*, an editorial declared that "the term 'colored' is not a good one. Whenever used, it recalls to mind the offensive distinction of color." T. Thomas Fortune, a leading journalist in the first quarter of the twentieth century, also declared that the word was a vague misnomer and had "neither geographical nor political significance, as applied to race" (as quoted in Berry and Blassingame 1982:391). Nevertheless, many people, especially middle- and upper-class African Americans, used the term "colored" (Isaacs 1964:70). The need for a name that was self-defined and descriptive remained.

The more recent resurgence of the term "people of color" is used by some to designate all people except those of European descent. Some people who identify themselves as Hispanic, but who can claim no African or Native American ancestry, refer to themselves as "people of color." The fact that some people who are Jewish also consider themselves to be "people of color" (Kaye 1996) clearly calls attention to the generalization of the term. This generalized usage also underscores the fact that the term erases significant historical experiences that distinguish cultural and racial groups.

PAN-AFRICAN CONNECTIONS

While the term "Black" resurfaced during the Black Power movement, "Afro-American" and "African" were also becoming more common. The use of these terms was, in part, an outcome of emerging African American and Black Studies departments that began on campuses across the country in the 1960s. It was in this context, as well as in non-university settings, that a large number of African Americans became more aware of African liberation struggles. That indigenous African movements were concomitant in time, and to a certain degree in nature, to civil rights movements in the United States, brought about greater affinity between indigenous and diaspora Africans.

Even before pan-Africanism became popular in the Western Hemisphere, Queen Mother Moore (nee Audley Moore, 1898–1997), a veteran activist for African American and women's self-determination, campaigned for women's rights and African liberation. A follower of Marcus Garvey, Moore recognized the cultural significance of names when she asserted that

Negro is a terrible word. I am responsible for our people putting down that word. I'm opposed to *black* too. Neither one indicates where you come from and both of them are used derogatorily. I thought that we should use *Africans*. We're African people. (Lanker 1989:103)

A small sector of African Americans consider themselves African. An even larger percentage have expressed their African identity in other ways, such as studying African languages, adopting African names, wearing African clothes, and keeping their hair in its natural form. Although these expressions are often represented in the literature as short-lived, superficial symbols, they remain in existence and are as significant now as they were in the 1960s in that they constitute a positive response to images that have been degraded since the beginning of American history.

PERSONAL NAMES

The use of African personal names by African American nationalist groups also underscores the perception of names and political ideology as coterminous. The eschewal of last names among members of the Nation of Islam (also known as Black Muslims) is most instructive. The Nation of Islam (NOI) is a "Black nationalist" group organized by Wali Fard in 1930. The general principles promoted by Fard and his successor, Elijah Muhammad (aka Elijah Poole), were freedom and justice for people of African descent.

In the early years of the organization, Elijah Muhammad promoted reparations and a separate territory (in Africa or the United States) for African Americans. The U.S. government was not forthcoming with reparations, but the organization managed to prosper with a proliferation of restaurants and other business enterprises. In addition, the popularity of the organization grew and membership catapulted with the emergence of Malcolm X in the 1960s. With the assassination of Malcolm X in 1965 and the death of Elijah Muhammad in 1975, the organization went through a lot of changes.[2] Nevertheless, the original ideology of the NOI promulgated pride in one's African American ancestry and an awareness of the history of Africans in America. The NOI was keenly aware of the damage done to our cultural integrity and sought to rectify this by addressing the importance of self-identification.

The Nation of Islam did this, in part, by replacing their European appellations, which they call slave names, with the letter X to underscore the loss of their original African family names. "X" serves at least a dual purpose. First, it represents the forced separation of African-descended people from their original families and then relocates all African Americans within the same family. Some members of the Nation of Islam adopt Muslim names in order to symbolize their Islamic beliefs. The Nation chooses to overlook the fact that Arabs preceded fifteenth-century Europeans in the enslavement of Africans (J. Harris 1971, 1974; Phillips 1985:66–87).

Members of other nationalist groups such as the Republic of New Africa (Obadeli 1972) also espouse African cultural revivalism which includes the adoption of new personal names, both Muslim and non-Muslim. This symbolic gesture coincides with their political orientation that has emphasized separation from European American society and/or reparations from the U.S. government for slavery and its aftermath (Kly 1985; Obadeli 1972; Robinson 2000; Van Deburg 1992:144–49; 302, 334).

Beginning in the 1960s, African Americans who were not affiliated with nationalist organizations began to shed their slave names and adopt African varieties (Malik-Khatid 1995:349–353). During this same period, increasing numbers of African Americans gave their children African names at birth.

Throughout history other African Americans who were not aligned with nationalist groups have given their children names that, while not African, are distinguished from European American names (Pharr 1993:400–409; Thompson 1995:30). There is a long and ever-changing list of these names that include, for example, LaTosha, LaToya, and Chante. Although these are not African names, they represent an effort to choose names that distinguish African American people as a distinct group. Lisa Jones (1994:18–19) refers to such names as the "Watts, Africa, aesthetic" and suggests that they "boldly announce themselves, [and] aim for the singular quality of royalty." Other studies indicate that some of these coined names may be derived from African names (Dunkling and Gosling 1983; Eagleston and Clifford 1945:57–64; Paustian 1978:177–191; and Puckett 1975).

NEGATIVE LABELS

Just as African Americans have differed in their opinions on representative names, they have also disagreed on the contextual meanings of racial epithets.

The schism arises between those who feel that the term nigger assumes positive connotations when used among African Americans and those who find it offensive under any circumstances.

Some African Americans routinely use the term "nigger" (or "nigga") in phrases such as, "That's my nigga" or "S/he's a baad nigga." This internal usage ostensibly gives the term a positive connotation. As Ottley (1968:279) remarks in *A New World A-Coming*, "the term nigger (when used by African Americans) sometimes [has] a good deal of affectionate meaning to [it]...." Even though certain sectors of the African American population claim that the internal use of this negative term lightens its original meaning, "it never really relieves it of its burden of contempt and self contempt" (Isaacs 1964:65). More important, when one listens to how African Americans use the term, it is clear that they usually use it disparagingly.

This usage is proliferated in rap lyrics, song titles, and in the names of rap groups, such as Niggaz with Attitudes. Even though some rap music is viewed as positive and progressive because of the social commentary, gangsta rap is most noted for its use of negative images of women and African American people by the consistent use of "bitch," "ho," and "nigga." Examples of this usage in song titles include "Niggas 4 Life" (Niggaz with Attitudes), "Strictly for My Niggas" (2 Pac) and "For All My Niggas and Bytches" (Snoop Doggy Dogg). In a National Public Radio interview, rap artist Ice T defended these practices with, "That's how we are...that's how we talk in the ghetto ... it's a Black thang." While this language may be common among some African Americans, it is not universally accepted (Kitwana 1995:26). In response to the rationalization offered by some African Americans who claim that "nigger" is neutralized when used internally, Haki Madhubuti (1994:36–37) writes that

There are certain words...that are debilitating to use, no matter how often they are used. Such a word is nigger.... A nigger, which is a pitiful and shameful invention of Europeans, cannot be de-stereotyped by using it in another context, even if the users are Black and supposedly politically correct (they are mostly young and unaware). A nigger is a nigger is a nigger and white folks love to hear us denigrate each other.

"Nigger" is fraught with the history of slavery and racism that spawned a litany of stereotypes characterizing African people as stupid, lazy, ugly, and dirty. Almost any disparaging characteristic that can vilify human beings is embodied in this term. Moreover, the ignominy that it conveys, its longevity and ubiquitousness, have placed a deep-seated and enduring stigma on African people that precludes any cleansing of the term even when used by African Americans. Instead of waging a revolution, as many rap singers and fans claim it does, gangsta rap language has the effect of further institutionalizing negative images of African American people. The internalization of these images has been closely studied (Clark 1965:63–64; Gettone 1981:311; Goodman 1964:46; 55–58; 60). As Delgado (1995) writes:

The psychological responses to...stigmatization consist of feelings of humiliation, isolation, and self-hatred. Consequently, it is neither unusual or abnormal for stigmatized
individuals to feel ambivalent about their self-worth and identity. (160)

CULTURAL AND POLITICAL MEANING OF NAMES

Other terms, such as "underclass" (Wilson 1978), "non-white," and
"minority" are commonly used without full consideration of their import and
impact. These terms render African Americans passive and establish "white"
as the relevant frame of reference (Fairchild 1985:53). "Minority" and
"underclass" connote insignificance and being downtrodden without naming
the people and circumstances that bring about these conditions—once again
blaming the victim.

Having a name to go by remains a central issue because African Americans
continue to be divided along cultural and political lines. With the postmodern
emphasis on race as a nonexistent category, it becomes more important to emphasize the significance of an African or African American identity, since without a nucleus grounded in cultural and historical experience we are destined to
build ephemeral identities based on others' conceptions of who we are. Con-
versely, recognizing ourselves as a people is both a precursor and a catalyst for
sustaining more broad-based struggles for political and economic equality.

Unfortunately, although many African Americans have died in their struggle for political and cultural integrity, there has not been a protracted cohesive
movement that has incorporated all sectors of the African American population. Since the 1960s, many middle-class African Americans have benefited
from civil rights acts, but the masses of African Americans remain poor and
otherwise manginalized. Rectifying this situation requires a mass movement at
national and international levels. It is for this reason that emphasizing the
African in African American is an important initial step in realizing this goal.
African Americans must be connected with the larger population of indigenous
and diaspora Africans throughout the world. The reality that many people of
African descent have been persuaded to eschew their Africanness complicates
this problem. That they are struggling for survival is yet another factor that
makes looking to future political and economic needs more difficult. Continental Africans, too, are embroiled in internecine struggles that overshadow al-
liances with diaspora Africans. These and other cultural and political factors
weigh against such a consolidation; nevertheless, the need remains.

In addition to Caribbean and African self-interests, there are other local
forces that impede this kind of centripetal force. African American scholars, for
example, William Wilson (1978) and Shelby Steele (1990), minimize the need
for race-based mobilization and enhance the power of European American
ideology that would erase race while practicing racism.

In the *Declining Significance of Race* (1978) Wilson claims that class has superseded race as the primary factor holding African Americans back. He suggests that:

To say that race is declining in significance...is not only to argue that the life chances of [B]lacks have less to do with race than with economic class affiliation but also to maintain that racial conflict and competition in the economic sector—the most important historical factors in the subjugation of [B]lacks—have been substantially reduced. (152)

Although Wilson concedes that a large sector of African Americans remain below the poverty line, he adroitly leaves this faction to struggle for subsistence and focuses on the middle class who, he says, are no longer "severely affected" by racial antagonism in the economic sector. Even though Wilson refers to opportunities that were available in the 1970s, he fails to point out that in every decade following the Civil War, the economic gap between African and European Americans has been considerable (see Hacker 1992:93–106). So even though Wilson is correct regarding the growing African American middle class, Hacker details this development with the following:

[In African American middle class families] more typically, the husband is likely to be a bus driver earning $32,000, while his wife brings home $28,000 as a teacher or a nurse. A white middle-class family is three to four times more likely to contain a husband earning $75,000 in a managerial position, which allows him to support a nonworking wife. It is not easy to visualize these two couples living on the same block, let alone becoming acquainted with one another (104–105).

Moreover, thirty-three percent of African Americans live below the poverty line—this figure has fluctuated only a few percentage points in the past several decades. In addition, middle-class African Americans still earn less and have less wealth than European Americans with equal levels of education and experience. These facts might lead one to believe that scholars like Wilson who have "made it" become purblind in the process and are unable to see the socioeconomic, psychic, and cultural damage that continues to plague African American communities.

In *The Content of Our Character* (1990), Steele attempts to erase the reality of racial discrimination, even more thoroughly by claiming that African Americans' economic, political, and psychological devastation is primarily their fault. He transforms the institutional racism that continues to marginalize African Americans into "residual racism" and asserts that "racism [has] receded, [and that] much of the problem must be of our own making (15)." Indeed, the pervasive theme in his book is that African Americans enjoy playing the victim because this gives them an excuse for not using opportunities that are omnipresent.

This view is regretful. While it is true that there are some African Americans who use the "race card" as a convenience, lack of effort on the part of some cannot explain the myriad forms of systemic racism that affect the opportunities of the majority. The legacy of slavery left many African American families with nothing but the clothes on their backs, if that. This lack of capital was handed down from one generation to the next. And to this was added mob violence and job discrimination, which prevented the masses of African Americans from buying the bootstraps as many of the populations that Steele praises have been able to do.

Thirty-three percent of African Americans live below the poverty line. Is Steele suggesting that millions of people of African descent are simply not trying? Given the history of racial discrimination in the job market, the impetus for such a view is puzzling. However, when one considers that moderate (at least that) African American male academics tend to be more readily accepted in European American-controlled institutions, this might provide at least a partial answer to Steele's confusion. In any event, it is this kind of historical amnesia that contributes to the retardation of African American progress.

Such progress will only come about as a result of a unified campaign against racism which, in part, will be predicated on our willingness to think of ourselves as a people and experience pride in this identity. That is, the degree of dissension over a name for people of African descent and the number of labels we have chosen over the decades is indicative of the instability of our identity as a people.

I suggest that whatever our terminology is, whatever it will be, it must be of our own choosing. By now, it is clear that my own preference is African American (or American African) because it locates Africans in America in time and space (Clarke 1986). In addition to claiming the same privileges as other groups in the United States, the term "African," designates our African ancestry and "American" speaks to our current citizenship status. The term is also a reminder of the insidious trade in human souls—an institution that many European Americans would rather pretend never happened. Given the continued systemic discrimination and alienation that many of us experience, perhaps a better term might be "American Africans." This thinking coincides with that offered by Fairchild (1985:54) when he suggests that of the terms mentioned above

"African-American" seems appropriate. Adoption of this term would serve at least four purposes. First, it would remove the ambiguity of the capitalization [or] noncapitalization issue. Second, it would formalize the "African Connection" and, perhaps, increase a consciousness in Pan-Africanism. Third, it could serve to attenuate whites' attitudinal hostilities [Although their behavioral hostilities are an entirely different question; see Longshore and Beilin (1980) in this connection]. Finally, it may serve to add dignity and self-respect to the people who adopt and use the term, with consequent effects on psychological well-being.

Although Fairchild's work in the area of naming is thorough and instructive, African Americans will have come a long way once they reach the point of being less concerned with how they are viewed by others, and more concerned with how they view themselves.

The vast majority of African Americans continue to refer to themselves as "Black," but many have recognized the importance of connecting names with a cultural experience that has its roots in Africa (Blauner 1972:146–155; Weisbord 1969:305–321). Since the 1960s, many African Americans have adopted the terms "African" and "African American." Even though this process of re-Africanization is still in its early stages, there are signs that the past is not

completely irreversible. In spite of the width of the Atlantic, [African Americans] may yet stretch out their arms towards each other, seeking to touch the gulf of the ocean and the chasm of history. (Mazrui 1986:113)

Since the 1950s, increasing numbers of African Americans have figuratively and literally traversed the Atlantic to settle in Africa (Lake 1995). Increasing numbers of African Americans are also making temporary visits to Africa. Those who have chosen to live their lives in the diaspora make manifest their African ancestry in a number of ways already mentioned.

On the face of it, these behaviors may seem unremarkable; however, given the large numbers of African American people throughout history who have repudiated their origins, these symbolic links are noteworthy.

As African Americans begin to embrace their African aspect, scholars and non-scholars alike have attempted to erase difference in the abstract while continuing to practice discrimination based on racial criteria. This camouflage lays the groundwork for proposing that African Americans can pull themselves up by their bootstraps, as did many European immigrants. Such proposals, which have existed since the end of slavery, ignore the barriers imposed by institutional discrimination, violence, and the psychic damage inflicted during slavery and its aftermath. In fact, even attempts to equate the experiences of Africans and Europeans in America erase the reality of slavery and its legacy, which is *the* factor that separates the African American experience.

NOTES

1. According to authors and observers of the time, Truth ostensibly asked, "ar'n't I a woman?" in a speech in Akron, Ohio. Although feminists have used this statement to galvanize their movements since the nineteenth century, it is uncertain whether she actually uttered these exact words. For more information on Truth and her historical speech, see Nell Painter (1996), Jean Yellin (1989) and Elizabeth Stanton, Susan B. Anthony, and Matilda Joslyn Gage (1883).

2. After Elijah Muhammad's death, religious and political differences splintered the Nation of Islam into several groups. Louis Farrakhan resuscitated the Nation of Islam, calling himself Elijah Muhammad's "national representative." Elijah Muhammad's son, Wallace D. Muhammad, formed his own group, the World Community of Al-Islam in the West. Other offshoots of the NOI include The Lost Found Nation of Islam, the Five Percent Nation of Islam, and the Allah Community. For more detailed information on the permutations of African American Muslims see (among others) Gardell (1996), El-Amin (1991), and Marsh (1984).

Chapter 2

Mulattoes and Color Consciousness in the United States

Since the sixteenth century, miscegenation between people of African and European descent has created a population of mixed-race people in all parts of the African Diaspora. In the United States, this population was produced in three ways—the European rape of African women, legal marriages, and consensual sexual relations outside of marriage. The European rape of African women, which began on slave ships and continued on the plantations, resulted in a lighter-skinned mulatto class that served as a buffer between African and European Americans. Because of their estrangement from the African American community, this mixed-race group caused a significant rift in cultural and political solidarity in North America as well as in other parts of the African Diaspora. During the slave era, mulattoes were often given their freedom, which afforded them economic and educational opportunities over their darker kin (Isaacs 1964:68; Keith and Herring 1991:760–778). This was especially so in Charleston, South Carolina, and New Orleans, Louisiana, where prosperous mulattoes sustained endogamous social and political communities.

Attention to these disparities within the African American caste system are important to better understand the way in which class was intricately tied to color. Moreover, the legacy of mulatto economic advantage was passed down to successive generations along with attendant cultural mannerisms and ideological beliefs. Where the literature does address divisions between mulattoes and other people of African descent, some scholars suggest that at the turn of the twentieth century, they ceased to exist. This claim requires further investigation and is taken up here and in succeeding chapters.

While miscegenation between European American women and African men was not unusual, the majority of mixed partners consisted of European men and African women. Many of these men were upper class who took advantage of slave women or who courted mulatto women. In some parts of the South, even with anti-miscegenation laws in place, mulatto women had open consensual affairs with European American men. Women among the *gens de couleur* of New Orleans, Louisiana, are most notable in this regard. In many cases, female slaves were forced into prostitution or concubinage by their masters, but open consensual relations were the order of the day. Not only did European men find these women exceptionally attractive, but the women fashioned themselves as superior to darker skinned people of African descent. The practice of miscegenation in Louisiana was so common that it developed into an institution known as placage.

In New Orleans, interracial affairs were institutionalized in "quadroon balls." These were regular and public affairs in which wealthy European American men formally courted prospective mulatto mistresses. When the man had made his choice, he met the woman and her mother to offer an arrangement, a placage, in which he agreed to maintain the woman in a certain style and provide for any children who might be born of the union (Williamson 1980:23). If the mother accepted the offer, the suitor established his consort in a home of her own. Often these women established their own businesses that outlasted their relationships with their European paramours. These liaisons were common between well-to-do men and quadroon women; however, such unions were initiated by men of all classes and nationalities. Foreign-born men from England, France, and Italy often courted quadroon women (Everett 1952: 234–235).

Some of these common-law marriages were short lived, others lasted until the death of one of the partners. The commonality of these unions is indicated in the following article in *The Washington Bee*:

WHITE MEN

IN LOUISIANA MARRYING COLORED WOMEN.

NEW ORLEANS, LA., SET. [*SIC*] 14, 1909.

"She's my wife. We have lived together 38 years. The law can not [sic] estrange us." Thus spoke Joseph Lawrence, a white farmer, in the second criminal court, while he was awaiting trial on the charge of marrying a colored woman. Through the arrest of Lawrence and his colored wife the police discovered a hard situation. All around Lee Station the white farmers and fishermen and other classes have intermarried with colored people and reared large families, regardless of the law against such. A number of arrests have been made, but it has been impossible to convict one for the reason that the white parties all went on the stand and swore they were colored. Just what the Prosecuting Attorney can do remains to be seen.

—The Picayune, New Orleans, La. (as quoted in *The Washington Bee* Oct. 23, 1909 Volume XXX:21.)

Mixed-race marriage had long been prohibited in New Orleans, but it occurred frequently enough that another bill was introduced into the legislature in February 1857 to outlaw marriages between people of European descent and anyone with "a taint of African blood."

Although Louisiana was noted for its interracial liaisons, it was not anomalous: European men in all areas of the South were known for seeking out women from among the *gens de couleur* who were mulattoes, octoroons or quadroons, people who were one-half, one-eighth, or one-fourth African, respectively.

The American folk song "The Yellow Rose of Texas" is but one testimony to the desire for mixed-race women. The version of this song that most baby boomers were compelled to learn in grade school is devoid of its original reference to a mulatto slave woman, Emily Morgan (Horton 1993:137, Turner 1976), because through the decades the lyrics have been changed.

The song was inspired by Morgan, who unwittingly played a decisive role in the defeat of General Antonio Lopez de Santa Anna y Perer de Lebron at San Jacinto. According to Turner (1976), Morgan was a slave owned by Colonel James Morgan, who bought her in New York and transported her to Texas in 1835. There she was captured by General Santa Anna, whom she served as a concubine. According to ethnologist William Bollaert, Sam Houston succeeded in a surprise attack in the battle of San Jacinto against Santa Anna, who was amorously engaged with Morgan. While Morgan may have led to the demise of Santa Anna's troops, she was also an inspiration for "The Yellow Rose of Texas," which has become integral to American folk music.

According to Turner (1976:49) the song was "composed and arranged expressly for Charles H. Brown by J. K. . . . Through the years the identity of the initialed composer or arranger has remained a mystery" (see original lyrics in Appendix E). Throughout the ensuing decades, writers have changed the lyrics, and after the 1858 and 1906 versions (see Appendices F and G), the term "darky" disappeared altogether, thus obliterating the metaphor of the yellow "rose." While lyrics can easily be changed, the historical accounts, and, indeed, the progeny of mixed unions cannot obscure the genetic record. Despite theories that promulgated the inferiority of African women, it was not unusual for European American men to engage in conjugal relations with these same women.

It is not surprising that the reactions of the wives to their husbands' affairs with African women were not benign. This was especially true if the women were mixed race. European American women were known to assault quadroon mistresses, heap scorn upon their husbands, and, in exceptional cases, sue for divorce. Because divorce was rarely countenanced in this era, European American wives had to endure their husbands' insults. In one case, however, where the husband brought his mistress to live under the same roof as his wife, she was granted a divorce (Everett 1952:236). An accounting of the varied responses by European American wives is best summarized by Gayarré:

The household peace was destroyed; there were secret tears, placid resignation, or open strife and deserved reproaches in the Caucasian homes. Sometimes there was an apparent ignorance of what it was better not to know; sometimes it was tolerated with indifference, or easy good nature, as an unavoidable evil, or as a temporary aberration in which the affections were not engaged. In such an incessant struggle the quadroons watched with mischievous keenness their more fortunate rivals whose rights of possession were guaranteed by the fist of church and state, and it is related that they systematically pursued a course of disparagement and slander toward them, and triumphantly exulted whenever any well founded censure could be bastened on any married white woman. (Gayarré 1879, as quoted in Everett 1952:236)

Unmarried European American men also kept mixed-race mistresses, often to the dismay of the latter's male relatives. But so intent were these women on engaging in these affairs that they would do anything, even sue their objecting fathers for slander (Everett 1952:237) to maintain these liaisons that not only increased their status, but that of their children as well. In some cases, what began as affairs ended in marriage.

Less frequently, European American women had sexual relationships with men of mixed or African descent—a practice that was much less tolerated than affairs between European men and African women. When they did occur, women were often given light jail sentences (usually six months). If the man was a slave, he might be given a whiplashing. If he was free, he might be imprisoned (Blassingame 1973:19). In African male and European female relationships, the more "respectable" the woman, the more European American society resisted these unions. In actuality, male slaves had sexual relations more often with European indentured servants[1] than with upper-class women.

Even though interracial unions were against the law during the slave era, there were a considerable number, especially in Maryland, Virginia, and Louisiana. The children of these unions in Virginia and in some other states were bound out by church wardens until the age of thirty. The servant woman guilty of having a mulatto child was sold for five years as a punishment (Reuter 1918:158).

The relative frequency of miscegenation in Louisiana was due primarily to a more relaxed racial atmosphere in antebellum New Orleans. This is not to suggest that slavery was benign in this region, or that mixed-race people were not discriminated against. The relatively lax environment did not obviate clear boundaries between Africans and Europeans. Schools, jails, hospitals, and other institutions were legally segregated. In addition, Africans could not vote and rape was a crime only when committed by an African. In spite of these realities, free people of African descent, most of whom were mixed race, were given more legal and social rights under French and Spanish rule than was the case in other colonies (Hirsch and Logsdon 1992:24). Free African Americans in New Orleans could carry guns, establish conjugal relations with slaves, and openly fraternize with Europeans in cafes and other public places.[2]

While laws were in place to keep people of African descent "in their place," free Africans regularly danced, gambled, drank, and copulated with whites (Blassingame 1973:9). This more tolerant attitude toward Africans in New

Orleans led slaves to be more insolent than their cohorts in others parts of the United States.

The degree of miscegenation is reflected in the numbers of free African Americans in Louisiana compared to other states (Hirsch and Logsdon 1992:209, n15). In 1860 there were 18,647 free African Americans in Louisiana, compared to 114 in Arkansas and 753 in Mississippi. Across the country, by 1860 488,000 Africans were free. Acts of manumission were granted as a result of military participation and faithful service. In some instances, slaves were able to buy their own freedom. These cases notwithstanding, the majority of freed Africans consisted of the progeny of European men and African women. Even though mulattoes were prevalent in Louisiana, they were ubiquitous throughout the United States.

In 1850 there were approximately 3,639,000 people of African descent in the United States. Out of this population, 406,000 were "visibly mulatto. Free mulattoes numbered 159,000, slave mulattoes 247,000" (Williamson 1980:24). Free mulattoes in the lower South were more numerous and prosperous than those in the upper South. While the majority of mulattoes in the lower South were slaves, many of the free and well-to-do mulattoes themselves owned slaves. As indicated in Table 2.1, after slavery the number of mulattoes in the United States increased.

The fact that the earliest slave laws in 1662 dealt with the disposition of mulatto children indicates that racial intermixture had occurred frequently and early in U.S. history. This was the case in northern as well as southern slave and non-slave states. In 1677 a European woman was indicted for having sexual relations with a slave (Turner 1911:29). In 1700 in Philadelphia, punishment for the rape of European American women by African men was death. By 1705, the punishment was reduced to whipping or branding—a code that was reserved only for African men. These punishments notwithstanding, racial mixture was frequent enough to provide impetus for a 1725 law that prohibited miscegenation. Despite sanctions against this practice, it was frequent enough in Pennsylvania that a settlement in Sussex County bore the name of "Mulatto Hall" (Turner 1911:29). By the time William Penn was ceded the colony in 1681, twenty percent of the African population was mulatto. Mulattoes were present in all areas of the United States in the early colonial period; however, their

Table 2.1
Increase in Mulatto Population

1870	1890	1910
584,000	1,132.000	2,050,000

Source: Compiled from Joel Williamson, 1980: *New People: Miscegenation and Mulattoes in the United States.* New York: Free Press, p. 112.

numbers in urban areas far exceeded those in rural areas. This was probably due to the fact that free African Americans tended in reside in larger cities. Urban mulattoes were more prominent in southern states, but as shown in Table 2.2, their preponderance was notable in northern cities as well.

Mulattoes often viewed themselves as more physically attractive based on their lighter skin, straighter hair, and sometimes European facial features. In some cases, European Americans felt that mulattoes were more mentally fit than other people of African descent and considered light-skinned men to be better leaders of African Americans' social and political pursuits. Mulattoes fancied themselves as superior to other people of African descent and fashioned themselves as "leaders of the race."

A number of European Americans thought that mixed-bloods were more intelligent than other people of African descent, but they did not think them equal, in any sense, to people of European extraction. Even though light-skinned people enjoyed social and economic advantages, European Americans defined racial categories in Black and White terms and discriminated against "light" and "dark" African Americans, giving preference to lighter-skinned people when it was to European American advantage. Nevertheless, mulattoes strove to emulate European Americans in appearance and social and political manners. The goal of many people in this category was to create a third caste system that would repudiate the bipolar racial categories that defined racial demography in the United States.

Color prejudice within the African American community was pervasive. Schisms were evident at every level—from the selection of friends to the formation of religious and social affiliations. These divisions were rife throughout the country, but were most notable in Louisiana and South Carolina. The mulatto population in Charleston, South Carolina, during the latter half of the eighteenth century was small in relative and absolute numbers (see Tables 2.3 and 2.4), but made its presence felt based on its economic power within the African community.

In antebellum North America and during Reconstruction, several mulattoes formed exclusive social organizations that, while sometimes charitable to poorer Africans, were adamant in their commitment to the maintenance of the color line within the African community. This was especially the case in South Carolina. At the suggestion of Reverend Thomas Frost, a European American rector of the St. Philip's Protestant Episcopal Church, James Mitchell with four other mulatto men formed the Brown Fellowship Society (BFS) on November 1, 1790, in Charleston, South Carolina. The BFS admitted "only brown men of good character who paid an admission fee of fifty dollars" (Frazier 1957:77). "Good character" meant light skin color and economic success. The Fellowship's motto was "Charity and Benevolence" and had among its goals to provide aid to widows and orphans or "our fellow creatures." The benevolence of this organization was mostly targeted to its own members and their families, which was in keeping with their racially segregated philosophy.

Table 2.2
Percentage of Mulattoes in Total African American Populations in Selected Cities

Area	1860
Georgia	
Savannah City	18.1
Rest of State	8.2
Jefferson Co. (Louisville) Louisiana	
New Orleans City	48.9
Rest of State	11.0
South Carolina	
Charleston City	25.2
Rest of State	5.5
Kentucky	
Jefferson County (Louisville)	21.8
Rest of State	20.0
Missouri	
St. Louis Country (St. Louis)	32.7
Rest of State	19.2
Virginia	
Richmond City	21.4
Rest of State	16.9
New York	
King's County (Brooklyn)	19.5 (N.Y. City 3.3)
Rest of State	20.3
Illinois	
Cook County (Chicago)	49.3
Rest of State	46.8
Massachusetts	
Suffolk Co. (Boston)	38.3
Rest of State	29.9

Source: U.S. Census, 1890: Population, Vol. 1, Part 1. Compiled by Reuter, 1918: *The Mulatto in the United States*. Boston: Richard G. Badger.

Table 2.3
Racial Demographics in Charleston, South Carolina: 1790

Descent	Population
European	8,089
African	7,684
Mulatto	586

Source: Compiled from Fitchett, 1940: The traditions of the Free Negro in Charleston, South Carolina. *The Journal of Negro History* 25(2): 139–152.

BFS members (see Appendix H) included tailors, carpenters, shoemakers, draymen, and butchers. In the late eighteenth and nineteenth centuries these occupations were considered prestigious for anyone with African ancestry and were absolutely so compared to the lot of African slaves. Indeed, many of Charleston's mulatto class owned slaves themselves and were also wealthy in real estate property.

Given the longevity of the BFS, the positions of prominence that most of its members held, and the degree of their isolation from the rest of the African community in Charleston, it is surprising that more information on this group is not readily available in any single source.[3]

Most BFS members made their living from practicing a trade, but many were also heavily involved in the political development of South Carolina. For example, Robert Carlos DeLarge, born a slave on 15 March 1842,[4] was an agent for the Freedmen's Bureau and was integral to the formation of the Republican Party in South Carolina. He participated in the writing of that state's constitu-

Table 2.4
South Carolina Africans and Mulattoes: 1850

	Slave	Free
Black	372,482	4,588
Mulatto	12,502	4,372

Source: J. D. B. de Bow, ed. Compendium of the Seventh Census of the United States, p. 83. Quoted from Marina Wikramanayake, 1966: *The Free Negro in Ante-Bellum South Carolina*. Doctoral Dissertation. University of Wisconsin.

tion and was a vocal and active member of South Carolina's legislature (Christopher 1976:98). These accomplishments notwithstanding, his electoral victories were marked by fraud and resulted in his being unseated from his post in the House of Representatives in 1873.

While serving as a Congressman, his allegiance to all people of African descent was equivocal: in one breath he espoused equality for everyone in "my race," yet in 1865 he signed a petition that attempted to disenfranchise "ignorant" people of both races (Foner 1996:61). Delarge was also one of the many BFS members who owned slaves. Even though some mulattoes fought for equal rights for all people, others were interested in the welfare of African Americans only insofar as their own positions of wealth and prestige were not jeopardized. This observation is contrary to the way in which other scholars (see, for example, Harris 1981:290) depict the Brown Fellowship Society, and other color-conscious mulattoes.

Although members of the Society were wealthy and had adopted the social norms of European American society, they were not totally accepted by the latter. This marginalization, indeed, may have provided the impetus for the formation of the organization. While members were insular in their business associations, attitudes, norms, and marriage practices, at the same time, they provided certain opportunities for the less fortunate.

In 1803 Brown Fellowship Society members established the Minor's Moralist Society (which lasted until 1847), which provided for poor people of African descent. Thomas Bonneau also set up a school (1803–1829) for people of African descent who were not members of the society. Even with their penchant for upholding racial boundaries, other mulattoes who were sympathetic to the cause assisted slaves in purchasing their freedom—this was, of course, before 1820, when a law was passed forbidding the freeing of any slaves. While some members of the BFS established institutions to assist slaves and other poor people of African descent, the majority was bent on focusing their largess among themselves. According to Wikramanayake (1973:88–89):

Distinctions of color and caste penetrated deeply into free black society, fissuring the group. The chasm separating the free black upper class from the lower orders, moreover, presented an almost insurmountable obstacle to the building of an organic community. With no real middle class to bridge the gap, the free black elite could barely touch the lower classes through organized acts of charity. Nor was its effort wholehearted. The upper-class free black did not wholly identify himself with the entire free black group. His whole way of life was a close approximation of that of the dominant white society toward which he aspired.

A small sector of well-to-do dark-skinned African Americans resented the detachment that mulattoes displayed. Consequently, in 1843, Thomas Small, started the Society of Free Dark Men (SFDM) (later called The Humane Brotherhood) for more prosperous free Africans and mulattoes. Even though the SFDM was less strict in terms of its color-coded membership, Small and other members of this group also owned slaves. Nevertheless, the SFDM established the Eurphrat Society that was open to all people of African descent. The purpose of this Society was to "alleviat[e] the couch of pain, and helping a Brother when distressed" (as quoted in Harris 1981:296). Like the BFS, the Society of Free Dark Men established schools for their members' children (Powers 1994:50), had its own burial ground, and attended church separately from the majority of lighter-skinned African Americans. Similarly, it also served as a mutual aid society and supported family members in times of sickness and death. Even though the Society of Free Dark Men scorned the practices of the BFS, they were insular and endogamous like their nemesis. They owned land and tended to sell parcels of land only to members of their group and married within their class. Some also owned slaves.

Even in the face of these race and class divisions, some scholars (for example, Robert Harris 1981) argue that Charleston did not have a three-tiered racial hierarchy that characterized other states and the Caribbean. I suggest that even though Charleston's European American community did not make sharp distinctions between mulatto and African, mulattoes did. South Carolina's mulattoes in general, and in the Brown Fellowship Society in particular, married within their own class and color lines, they had their own burial plots, established their own schools, and worshiped in their own churches (when they did not worship with European Americans). In general, they thought of themselves as superior to darker African Americans and stayed to themselves. While some of their benevolent activities benefited Africans of all stripes, several scholars note that they regarded darker Africans with disdain. Their economic status alone created a substantial chasm between the mulatto elite and their darker kin.

Members of the Brown Fellowship Society were well off in relative and absolute terms compared with other African Americans of the period. Most members were involved in politics and real estate investment and acquired large sums of money from these enterprises. As discussed in Fitchett (1940:86), out of the 353 free Africans who owned land in 1859, only nine persons paid taxes on real estate valued over $10,000. According to Frazier (1966:149), 258 "free persons of color ... were paying taxes on real estate valued at a million dollars and 389 slaves." Slave owners were prominent among BFS members.

This is important to emphasize because some scholars (see, for example, Harris 1981:300; Wikramanayake 1973:40; and Woodson 1924) suggest that these individuals held slaves in order to allow them a greater measure of freedom than they otherwise would have enjoyed. At face value, this proposal seems attractive, if for no other reason than to assuage the sensibilities of African Americans and others who might find it difficult to come to terms with internal oppression.

But these sentiments cannot erase the fact that slaves owned by people of African descent were slaves. If it had been in the interest of their owners to allow them greater measures of liberation, a better solution would have been to set them free. It is important to note that there were free Africans and mulattoes who bought their relatives only for the purposes of freeing them from the control of their European American owners, and not for the purpose of economic gain. This notwithstanding, other Africans and mulattoes purchased slaves in order to augment their economic wealth. These slaves were considered and used as property, just as they were under European American ownership.

Slaveholding was practiced by African American men and women, the latter being more frequently emancipated. In 1850 free mulattoes consisted of 48.7 percent of the free population, yet "comprised 83.1 percent of the Afro-American slaveholders in South Carolina" (Koger 1985:29). In other states as well—in addition to other parts of the African Diaspora—slaveholding by people of African descent was not uncommon. In Mississippi, Virginia, and Louisiana slaveholding was more widespread, but people of African descent in all of the southern states owned slaves (Berlin 1979:273–279; Wilson 1912:483–494; Jackson 1968:205–229).

Harris (1981:290) suggests that a "careful analysis of the Brown Fellowship Society...raised enough doubt to question whether color consciousness was the prime variable in social relations among Charleston's free Afro-Americans." He goes on to imply that slaves owned by African Americans were not treated as property, but the historical record tells a different story. This record includes family wills that expose the nature of African American slave ownership:

I give and bequeath unto my Son Emanual forever my Negro boy slave named Joe. I also give and bequeath unto Said Son for life my Negro boy slave named Tom and immediately after the death of my said Son, should the said Negro boy have conducted himself toward my Said Son as a faithful servant, then I direct that he be emancipated, but should he not have conducted himself then I give the said Negro boy to such person as my said Son nominate and appoint in his last will and writing. (As quoted in Fitchett 1940:146 from Record of Wills, Vol. 36, Book C, 1818–1826, p. 1125)

Likewise Thomas S. Bonneau, a wealthy BFS member and a schoolteacher, stipulated in his last will and testament that his slaves, Scipio, Fanny, and Mary, should be sold to a Kentucky slave trader if they were obstreperous and non-compliant to his wife's demands (Koger 1985:98):

I desire that soon after my decease instruction shall be given to have all my stock and other things appertaining to my plantation in the country together with the plantation itself sold and the money arising from the same shall go to defray all expenses, taxes & provided however the said plantation cannot be sold at a fair price and it can be worked by the hands now there viz. Scipio, Abram and Peggy so as to pay expenses taxes and so forth in such case the same shall not be sold but retained for the benefit of the family if at all event, the Negroes on said plantation whose names are above mentioned be disposed of there shall be an exception If Scipio whom it is my wish shall be trained together with my slaves in town viz.: Fanny and Mary to be subservient to the wishes of my beloved wife Jennet Bonneau and children. (Vol. 39, Book C, 1826–1834, p. 905)

Bonneau, a BFS member from 1813 through 1831, clearly did not purchase slaves out of benevolence, but profited from the labor of several slaves on his properties in St. Thomas and St. Dennis Parishes. Between 1822 and 1830 alone he purchased slaves valued at $4,120, a very large sum of money for the time. During this same time period, he sold two slaves for $620. On April 23 he purchased a Negro girl named Betsey for $230. Later, after becoming displeased with the slave girl, he sold Betsey to Joseph Dereef (also a BFS member), a free man of color, for $270. Mr. Bonneau not only discharged his troublesome slave within two weeks of the date of purchase but made a profit of $40 (Koger 1985:98).

Richard Dereef, another prominent BSF member, was respected by European American aristocracy based on his support for Democratic agendas (Democrats being the far right group in the nineteenth century). Dereef was a man of considerable wealth, which included Dereef's Wharf, which he sold to the South Carolina Railroad in 1871.

A sizable portion of BFS members were slave owners (see Appendix I). One who became quite prosperous was Richard Holloway. In 1842 Holloway, the thirty-fourth Brown Fellowship member, drew up his will and left two of his slaves, Cato and Betty, to his wife (Schweninger 1990:102). No doubt these and other Holloway slaves contributed to the success of the Holloway Harness Shop (see Figures 2.1 and 2.2) and other enterprises that were passed down

Figure 2.1
J. H. Holloway Harness Shop. Courtesy of the Avery Institute, Charleston, South Carolina.

Figure 2.2
J. H. Holloway Business Card. Courtesy of the Avery Institute, Charleston, South
Carolina.

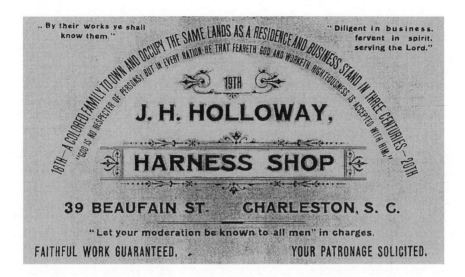

through the generations. The fact that slaves were handed down like so many
heads of cattle is testimony to their lot as chattel.

Mulatto slave ownership, in general, existed in South Carolina from the
eighteenth to the nineteenth century. Tables 2.5 and 2.6 indicate the numbers
of African American slaves and slave owners.

Other areas had considerably fewer slave owners of African descent, but they
were present throughout the state. People of African descent also separated
families and sold their slaves to European Americans. These chattels performed
various tasks, including rice, cotton, and tobacco cultivation, which added to the

Table 2.5
Number of Slaves Held by Free Black Slave Owners and Slave-Holding
Heads of Family in Charleston, South Carolina, 1790–1860

1790	1800	1810	1820	1830	1840	1850	1860
277	315	143*	1030	2195	2001	1087	544

Source: U.S. Department of Commerce, Bureau of Census, Eighth Census of the United States,
1790–1860; Schedule I & II, South Carolina, Tax List of Charleston City for 1860.
*Partial return for Charleston District.
Larry Koger, 1985: *Black Slave Owners: Free Black Slave Masters in South Carolina, 1790–1860*.
Jefferson, North Carolina: McFarland and Co., p. 21.

Table 2.6
Numbers of Free Black Slaveowners and Slave-Holding Heads of Family in Charleston, South Carolina

1790	1800	1810	1820	1830	1840	1850	1860
49	36	17	206	407	402	266	137

Source: U.S. Department of Commerce, Bureau of Census, Eighth Census of the United States, 1790–1860; Schedule I & II, South Carolina, Tax List of Charleston City for 1860 as cited in Koger 1985:20.

economic wealth and prestige of their owners. Clearly these written testimonies call into serious question the claim that African American slave owners held their human property for benevolent reasons. Even though the social status of African slaves and freed people of African descent differed greatly, European Americans made sure that freed people did not enjoy the privileges exclusive to the dominant society.

In fact, many European Americans resented the fact that "free Negroes" could move about without badges or certificates. In order to curtail the numbers of free African Americans, the dominant society set in motion legal prohibitions that would galvanize their safety and their hegemonic position. In 1794 a law was passed forbidding free Africans from entering South Carolina. This law was expanded in 1800 to prohibit the influx of slaves from other states.

In 1820 the general assembly prohibited any further emancipation of slaves without approval of the legislature. Because some slave masters tried to circumvent this rule and free certain slaves for "good behavior," the legislature strengthened its ruling in 1841, closing any loopholes. As a result owners could free their slaves only under extreme circumstances, as for example, a slave betraying plans of an insurrection. But even this often was not enough to emancipate a slave (Jones, N. 1990:71).

Even though more mulattoes enjoyed nominal freedom compared to other African Americans, European Americans of all economic classes went to great lengths to keep the distinctions clear between "White" and "Black." The legislature placed restrictions on Africans' movement in and out of the state. Africans also had to account for any prolonged period of absence outside of Charleston. In 1822 (the same year as the Denmark Vesey conspiracy) a bill was introduced into the legislature to expunge free Africans who had entered South Carolina in the past five years. The impetus for this and other restrictions was fear of economic competition from hired slaves and free Africans. In addition to the threat of skilled competition, the Denmark Vesey conspiracy, the Stono Rebellion, and other uprisings around the country instilled fear in the hearts of most European Americans who sought to galvanize the slave system (Powers 1994:62–63; Wood 1974.). Toward these ends, they enacted numerous laws in efforts to control the movements of free people of African descent, mixed race or otherwise. A free African was

tried for crime[s] before the same kind of court as that provided for the trial of slaves; he was subject to the same kind of penalties—corporal punishment—with the possible addition of a fine; his testimony could not be accepted in court against a white person, though a slave was a competent witness against a free [N]egro; [but] he had full right to acquire, hold and transfer property; he might and did often own slaves. (Henry 1914:180)

Even though these laws applied to all free Africans, the most affluent were able to solicit the support of sectors of the European American elite. During the Civil War, members of the Brown Fellowship Society made clear their commitment to the dominant class when they petitioned the governor, extolling the white blood running through their veins and assuring him that they would sacrifice their lives in defense of South Carolina. Evidently, these exhortations were effective, especially because a number of free people of African descent wholeheartedly supported the institution of slavery.

European Americans naturally supported the right of freed people to own slaves because this practice galvanized racism and gave freed people a stake in perpetuating the institution of slavery. Ironically, even though freed mulattoes cast their identities with people of European descent, they were not really free. In addition to the proscriptions noted above, every free person with any measure of African heritage was obliged to secure a European American guardian who could vouch for the good character of his charge. Figure 2.3 is a replica of a guardianship petition for Jehu Jones, a prominent BFS member who made the bulk of his wealth as a hotelier. Even though guardianship laws were not strictly enforced, their purpose was to keep intact and to make obvious the ranking within the racial hierarchy and to reiterate the inferiority of the African presence. In effect, the guardian was to freed men (women are not discussed in the literature in this regard) what the master was to the slave.

While divisions between mulattoes and Europeans persisted, BFS members went through great pains to endear themselves to their oppressors. In efforts to stay within the good graces of the European Americans, the Society made it clear in their bylaws that they were not a political group intent on addressing any of the overarching problems faced by people of African descent. The bylaws stated, in part, that:

All debates on controverted points of divinity or matters of the nation, governments, states or churches, shall be excluded from the conversation of this Society, and whoever shall presume to persist in such debate or argument, after admonition and objection be made by the chief officer, they shall be fined in a sum at the discretion of the Society. (Brown Fellowship Society Rules and Regulations, (Rule XVIII) p. 12)

At the time, there was a law on the Charleston books that not more than seven "Negroes" could assemble in public at one time. Because of the Society's

Figure 2.3
Guardianship Petition for Jehu Jones. South Carolina Department of Archives and
History. *Jehu Jones: Free Black Entrepreneur.* Courtesy of the Avery Institute,
Charleston, South Carolina.

To the Honorable the President & Members of the Senate of South Carolina:

The humble Petition of John L. Wilson, Sheweth: That he is Guardian to a

Coloured man named Jehu Jones; that the said Jehu Jones has always borne an

Irreproachable character; that as a member of society and the father of a family, he is

respected by all who know him; and that his wife and family being now abroad and

prevented from returning to this State, under the penalty of the late act, the said John L.

Wilson, for and in behalf of this ward, the said Jehu Jones, humbly prays your honorable

Body to permit the said Jehu Jones to visit his family in New York, and to return to this

State, by and with the Consent of your honorable body. And the said John L. Wilson, as

Guardian to the said Jehu Jones, assures your honorable body, that his ward is a fit and

Proper subject for the exercise of your Clemency, and is a worthy and respectable

Member of Society.

And your Petitioner will ever pray.

John L. Wilson

Columbia Decem. 6th 1823

---

ultraconservative agenda, European American authorities praised them and
exempted them from this law. The self-imposed injunction to be apolitical was
exercised on at least one other historical occasion which unequivocally marks
mulatto allegiance to European Americans and their commitment to mulatto
ascendency.

In 1822 Denmark Vesey, a freed African-born person, planned one of the
largest slave revolts in the history of North America. Vesey had convinced
more than nine thousand slaves that armed insurrection was their only hope
for freedom. William Paul, a Vesey recruit, attempted to convince Peter Desverneys, a mulatto slave, to join their ranks. Because Desverneys' master was un-
available at the time, he reported Vesey's plans to William Penceel, a member of
the Brown Fellowship Society (*Atlantic Monthly* 1861). Penceel encouraged

Desverneys to report the incident to his master, J. C. Prioleau, which he did. As would be expected, as word spread, free mulattoes and European Americans became alarmed and moved to dismantle Vesey's plans.

The conspiracy was soon unraveled and Vesey and several of his men were executed. In return for his dutiful service, Desverneys was granted his freedom and given a pension of $50 per year for the rest of his life. Once Desverneys was manumitted, he bought slaves himself. Clearly, this was not an example of benevolence because he later sold the son of Alfred and Lavinia Sanders, two of his slave servants.

William Penceel's reward was $1000 and exemption from paying the "free Negro" capitation tax that all other free African and mulatto persons were bound to pay (Fitchett 1940:147; Koger 1985:176). Pinceel's actions were also condoned by other BFS members who made no motions to expel him from the group. "While many within the slave community viewed [him] as an enemy and a traitor, he remained a respected and honorable man to the mulatto elite and the white citizens of Charleston City ... [who] perceived him as a safe Negro" (Koger 1985:180). That slaves and free African Americans across the country gave away plans of slave insurrectionists was not unusual. That individuals who acted to support the racist status quo were rewarded for these transgressions is instructive insofar as contemporary behaviors bring the same consequences. Ironically, while free mulattoes and Africans sought to protect the interests of the dominant class, they remained subject to the whims of the European American power structure, just as slaves were (Wood 1974).

In spite of this, the Brown Fellowship Society and other mulattoes in South Carolina looked upon darker-skinned people with disdain—a phenomenon that existed throughout the African Diaspora. The Brown Fellowship Society was joined by another antebellum organization, the Friendly Moralist Society. Like its predecessor, Moralist Society potential members were recommended by incumbents and were subject to a vote by the entire organization. Not only were race and color essential qualifications, but applicants were also scrutinized for their moral character and class affiliation. Membership guidelines stipulated that a prospective member must be a bona fide free brown man, over the age of eighteen, of moral character, and of good standing in the community.

"Should it be charged and proven that any member is not a bona fide free brown man, he shall immediately be expelled; and each of his recommenders shall be fined two dollars" (Rules and Regulations of the Friendly Moralist Society, Charleston, 1848). They even refused membership to mulattoes who associated with darker-skinned African Americans (Johnson and Roark 1982:248–249). African Americans were also excluded on the basis of occupation and unmixed heritage.

Brown Fellowship Society members consisted of more elite and older men than did members of the Friendly Moralists. Most members in the Brown Fellowship Society were propertied and lived in a more exclusive part of town. By contrast, the majority of Moralists did not own real estate and lived in an area of Charleston known as the Neck (see Curry 1981:63). These differences notwithstanding, the groups were coterminous in their racial philosophies and ideals. Moreover, as members of the Friendly Moralists rose in economic stature, they became members of the Brown Fellowship Society.

While a number of "mixed-blood" societies were short lived, the Brown Fellowship society lasted for more than a century. E. Horace Fitchett's (1940:145) treatment of this group indicates that there were still vestiges of the organization in the 1940s but that it soon died out; however, during my visit to Charleston in May 2001, I learned that the Society still exists although they are not as color conscious as they once were.

In 1890 the society changed its name to the Century Fellowship Society. In the early twentieth century wives and other relatives formed the Daughters of the Century Fellowship Society, the women's auxiliary arm of the Brown Fellowship Society. In keeping with the times, the Daughters did not have as its agenda the struggle for women's rights, but rather the advancement of the men's accomplishments. The objective of this branch was to erect "a hall to the memory of the men who won a page in the social history of the eighteenth century" (The Holloway Scrapbook).

Other actors involved in similar institutions included Charles Wilder, state representative from Richland, and president of the Friendly Union Society founded in 1852, and Henry Cardozo, senator from Kershaw, a member of the Bonneau Society. Still other light-skinned people found ways of distancing themselves from the rest of African America.

In the nineteenth and twentieth centuries, people of mixed descent continued to form exclusive groups. While many of these organizations did not include a color requirement as part of their written charter, it was implicit that membership in these groups was open only to people of lighter skin. Such individuals continued to curry favor with the European American community as well. This subject is taken up in more detail later. While some African Americans were striving for a closer fit within European American society, others attempted to distance themselves as far as possible.

AFRICAN AND CARIBBEAN MIGRATION

While the majority of people of African descent struggled or simply hoped for freedom, and free mulattoes tended to side with European American society, others had had enough of European racial hegemony and sought to emigrate to anywhere outside of America. Africa was their first choice. This movement began in the eighteenth century when eighty Boston Africans petitioned the state legislature for funding to repatriate. Throughout the eighteenth and nineteenth centuries other African Americans petitioned local and state governments for reparations for the purpose of repatriating back to Africa. Others formed their own organizations and attempted to migrate home (see Bittle and Geiss 1964; Blyden 1967; Drachler 1975; Esedebe 1982; Redkey 1969; Shick 1980; Uya 1971).

In 1816 a group of prominent European Americans[5] calling themselves the American Colonization Society (ACS) petitioned the federal government for funds to send Africans in America to Liberia. While many Africans and mulattoes wanted to emigrate, their motivations were different from those of the ACS, who were interested in ridding the United States of free Africans (Ferkiss 1966:292; Weisbord 1973:12–13). The fear was that they would incite enslaved Africans to rebel—a concern that plagued the European plantocracy throughout the slave era.

Many Africans, free and slave, strongly objected to repatriation efforts, asserting that they had shed their blood for America, that they had become part of its fabric, and would struggle for their freedom in the land they had come to know as home. But others went gladly. Between 1822 and 1867 the ACS shipped more than 18,000 people back to Africa (Liebenow 1969:8). Other diaspora Africans from the Caribbean were also taken to Africa under ACS auspices, including five hundred Jamaicans (mostly maroons) who were shipped to Nova Scotia and then Sierra Leone in 1800. Again, the impetus for Europe's role in these ventures was to make the island of Jamaica safe for European suzerainty. Insurrectionary Bajans (Barbadians) were exiled to Sierra Leone in 1819 for similar reasons (Fyfe 1962:136, 147, 291).

Many diaspora African repatriates in West Africa felt themselves a cut above their indigenous kin and considered Africans to be heathens just as European slaves traders and explorers did, and exploited them for their land and labor. In spite of this, there were well-known returnees who advocated that diaspora Africans learn the ways of their African brothers and sisters. Among them was Edward Blyden from St. Thomas, Virgin Islands, who clearly articulated these ideas when he wrote:

Black people who have lived in civilized communities, where there are different races, know the disparaging views which are entertained of Negro people by their neighbors, and often, alas, by themselves. Negroes in such communities, experience the greatest imaginable inconvenience. They never feel at home. In the depth of their being they always feel themselves strangers, and the only escape from this feeling is to escape from themselves. It is painful in America to see the efforts which are made by Negroes to secure outward conformity to the appearance of the dominant race. (1967:76–77)

Blyden, along with Henry McNeal Turner, Paul Cuffe, Martin Delany, and Marcus Garvey, was among the more prominent advocates of cultural and economic pan-Africanism. Although these leaders spent a good part of their lives attempting to reunite diaspora Africans to their homeland, their plans faltered for a number of reasons; most important was the lack of adequate funds. If diaspora Africans had received reparations after slavery, as their masters did, they may have been more successful. As it was, many emigrants went to Africa with very little. This and the fact that the environment and infrastructure on the continent lead many to their deaths did not bode well for a full-blown repatriation movement. Many of those who survived attempted to return to the United States. In spite of these minority efforts to settle in the motherland, the majority of people of African descent were wedded to the Americas. But marriage within a hostile environment born in slavery proved difficult, at best.

BLUE VEINERS

Even after the Civil War, internecine color struggles persisted as Jim Crow laws became more entrenched. Lynchings increased and African Americans continued to work the soil and reap few of its benefits. Economic advancement was further curtailed by a peonage system that kept African Americans beleaguered and indebted to former slave masters. Under this system, landless African Americans were compelled to rent land, tools, and animals in order to produce crops for sale and subsistence. But high rents and fixed scales left African Americans empty-handed at the end of the day. Thus, while European Americans were forceful and singular in their siege upon African people, African Americans weakened their own efforts for de facto freedom due to fissions around issues of class and color. Even the African American church, which served as the locus for organizing freedom movements, operated within a color caste system (Frazier 1963:31).

In 1870, the Colored Methodist Episcopal Church split off from the African Methodist Episcopal Church based on color hierarchy. This appellation was only changed from "Colored" to "Christian" in 1954. Color-conscious congregations existed in many parts of the United States and usually used a lightness test to determine who was eligible for admittance. In some churches, African Americans were subject to the bag test which involved placing an arm inside a brown paper bag. Only if the skin on the arm was lighter than the color of the bag would a prospective member be invited to attend church services. Other churches painted their doors a light shade of brown, and anyone whose skin was darker than the door was politely invited to seek religious services elsewhere. And in still other houses of worship throughout Virginia and in such cities as Philadelphia and New Orleans,

a fine-toothed comb was hung on a rope near the front entrance. If one's hair was too nappy and snagged in the comb, entry was denied. (Russell, Wilson, and Hall 1992: 27–28)

In Nashville, Tennessee, the First Congregational Church was known as a blue-vein institution or as "the B.V. church" (Robbins 1980). In Savannah, Georgia, St. Stephen's Episcopal Church was known as a color-coded institution dominated by light-skinned aristocrats. In 1872, when a near-white vestryman attempted to exclude all dark-skinned people from the church, J. Robert Love, a dark-skinned member of the congregation, strongly objected to this proposal and ultimately, along with other African Americans, formed their own St. Augustine Church. It was not until 1943 that the two congregations merged to form St. Matthews church.

St. Thomas African Episcopal Church in Philadelphia, the first African Episcopal church in the United States, was another example of a church that rose out of African American expungement from a European American congregation; in this case, St. George's Methodist Episcopal Church. St. Thomas soon formed the Sons of St. Thomas, whose constituents were elite members among Philadelphia's most well-to-do African Americans.

There were many such churches throughout the country, but, according to Gatewood (1990:281),

Few if any other [B]lack Episcopal congregations acquired a reputation for exclusiveness equal to that of St. Marks in Charleston, South Carolina. Founded in 1865 by fair-complexioned people of color who were freed before the Civil War, St. Mark's was for years the center of a controversy prompted by its effort to obtain representation in the Diocesan convention of South Carolina.

Among its founders were prominent families such as the Bennetts, McKinlays, Holloways, Dereefs, and Kinlochs, among others. The exclusive character of elite society was indicated by the fact that many of the members of St. Mark's were also members of the Brown Fellowship Society. St. Mark's did not allow anyone who was not an octoroon to become a member. St. Thomas Episcopal Church in Chicago, the Episcopal Church in Arkansas, All Saints' Church in St. Louis, and St. Phillips Church in Omaha, Nebraska, were also elitist, colorist, and nepotistic. The racial makeup of these organizations was not only reflected in skin color, but in the substance and tenor of the services as well. The mannerisms, dress, and music were more sedate and more like European American services.

For decades following slavery, mulattoes continued their endogamous patterns and formed private clubs to consolidate their social and political privilege (Russell, Wilson, and Hall 1992:24–26). Among these were the Orpheus Glee Club, the Monocan Club, and the Bon Ton Society in Washington, D.C. With the exception of the Bon Ton Society, which had formal rules regarding color, color-coded membership rules were tacitly instituted. Membership requirements made it such that only the upper class could join. That most of the upper class were mixed-race and tended to be insular in their social relations was well-known.

The Blue Vein Society, organized in Nashville, Tennessee (1889), was another organization primarily based on skin color. The rules for inclusion left nothing to the imagination because the

applicant had to be fair enough for the spidery network of purplish veins at the wrist to be visible to a panel of expert judges. Access to certain vacation resorts, like the Highland Beach on Chesapeake Bay, was even said to be restricted to blue-vein members. (Russell, Wilson, and Hall 1992:25)

In spite of its importance to African American historiography, very little substantive work has been written on the BVS and similar organizations.[6] Whether scholars thought that this beacon of racial exclusiveness was unimportant or whether they did not want to fully expose the internal color hierarchy in African America is unclear.

After the formation of the Blue Vein Society in Tennessee, "blue veinism" became a generalized term used by darker-skinned African Americans to refer to mixed-bloods who thought themselves superior. Mulattoes in other cities also formed exclusive organizations that consolidated social and economic privilege among its members. While they may not have referred to themselves as "blue vein," the character of their clubs reflected the attitudes and practices of the Nashville group. So common were these societies that a reiteration of their policies and sentiments often appeared in nineteenth and early twentieth century novels written by mulattoes, other people of African descent, and European Americans (see, for example, Tourgée 1890 and Hughes 1979).

Detroit was another city where color clearly marked people of different classes within the African American community. Detroit's "cultured colored" families regularly intermingled with Whites in political organizations, reform clubs, and small business ventures while their social activities moved parallel to but independent of White society (Fishel 1980).

Many members of the elite in major cities were well educated, light-skinned, professional people who were teachers, lawyers, doctors, or small businessmen. Other nouveau riche included barbers, servants, stewards, and waiters who acquired their wealth from the large tips doled out in private clubs, steamboats, and the like. Many of these mulattoes lived ostentatiously and soon ran out of cash and so died in poverty. Many mulatto elites with old money were public figures who made a name in African American historiography through their work in politics, business, or literature.

Charles Waddell Chesnutt (1858–1932) was one of the more prominent authors who focused on the vicissitudes of the internal color line. His specific reference to blue veiners and the plight of the mulatto can be found in his short stories, including *The Wife of His Youth and Other Stories of the Color Line* (1967) and *The House Behind the Cedars* (1900). Although he wrote sensitively and sometimes derisively about these issues, he himself was a member of the Social Circle in Cleveland, Ohio—a city that was at the pinnacle (or, if you wish, the nadir) of colorism. Along with the Chestnutts were other prominent individuals of the Circle including John Green, Leon Wilson, John Hope, and Powhattan Henderson. These and other mulattoes in Cleveland, Cincinnati, and Columbus held themselves aloof from other African Americans and rarely took part in their social or political affairs. When not cavorting among themselves, they took great pains to join European American religious and secular institutions. Sometimes to their dismay, they were rejected from these arenas because in the eyes of European Americans, they were inextricably tied to those who were more obviously African (Gerber 1976:133).

Other organizations that were virtually limited to light-skinned members (or brown-skinned people whose economic credentials compensated for their skin color), included the Douglass Literary Society (Columbus, Ohio); the Kingdom, the Lotus Club, and the 400 (Washington, D. C.); and the Manasseh Society in the Midwest. While this list of organizations is not exhaustive, it is indicative of the proliferation of such groups around the country.

It is important to note here that most African Americans, regardless of skin color, have assumed European American cultural habits—this has been the case since the days of slavery. At the same time, we have maintained and developed our distinctive cultural habits and identities. What is significant here is that a proportion of mixed-race people have always seen themselves as a cut above the rest, and have been endogamous in their social and kinship relations. In an *Ebony* magazine article (1955:55), "Negro Blue Bloods," the "brown aristocracy" continued to keep to themselves in family matters, social gatherings, and other milieu. That class was positively correlated with light skin is made clear in other *Ebony* articles, including "Society Rulers of 20 Cities" (1949:62–66) and "America's Ten Best-Dressed Negro Women" (1953:32–35).

At the dawn of the twenty-first century, class is less frequently correlated with the degree of African ancestry; however, a significant correlation persists (see Keith and Herring 1991:760–780). In social matters there is ample evidence that color remains a major factor within the African American community in matters of mate selection and the formation of criteria for beauty standards. I take this topic up in more detail in the following chapters.

"COLOR BLIND" LEGAL ENVIRONMENT

As debates and tensions persisted within the African American community, European American racism continued at ideological and legal levels. Resistance to this state of affairs was consistent throughout slavery in America and continued after its demise. One of the signature cases that characterized the postbellum era was *Homer Adolph Plessy vs. The State of Louisiana*, popularly known as *Plessy vs. Ferguson*). This case is relevant not only because it characterizes the racial climate of the day, but for its instructiveness on the complexity of color consciousness among European and African Americans. This landmark case is well recorded, thus only a brief outline is necessary here.

On June 7, 1892, Homer Plessy, a shoemaker from New Orleans, was incarcerated for sitting in a "White Only" railroad car of the East Louisiana Railroad. Plessy took the case to court and argued that the Separate Car Act violated his Thirteenth and Fourteenth Amendment rights. John Howard Ferguson, a lawyer from Massachusetts who adjudicated the case, decided that the state had a right to uphold the Separate Car Act on interstate travel. Plessy appealed to the state Supreme Court, where Justice Henry Brown upheld Ferguson's decision. The language in his decision clearly demonstrates the power of white privilege to reinterpret the law in ways that worked to majority advantage. Brown declared that the Separate Car Act does not conflict with the Thirteenth Amendment since it had

no tendency to destroy the legal equality of the two races. ... The object of the [Fourteenth Amendment] was undoubtedly to enforce the absolute equality of the two races below the law, but in the nature of things it could not have been intended to abolish distinction based upon color, or to enforce social, as distinguished from political equality, or a comingling of the two races upon terms unsatisfactory to either.

The only dissenter in the case, Justice John Harlan, emphasized that the Constitution was intended to be color-blind and that "in respect to civil rights, all citizens are equal before the law." For decades to come, Harlan's words fell on deaf ears in the South and other parts of the country and African Americans had yet to enjoy the freedoms promised by the Reconstruction Amendments. Moreover, *Plessy vs. Ferguson* effectively redoubled the effects of the 1883 constitutional amendment that overturned the 1875 Civil Rights Act that declared public accommodations equally available to all citizens. With their ability to change state and constitutional law at their discretion, European Americans extended their dominance and white-skin privilege.

What is even more interesting about Plessy's case for our purposes here is that Homer Plessy was not outraged because the rights of African Americans were once again abrogated. Instead, his concern was that he was not regarded as a European American. He was an octoroon, seven-eighths European and one-eighth African descent. He argued that property was considered part of citizenship and that his European genealogy was property. Even though Plessy had been living as a European American and looked visibly "White," the court considered him to be a person of African descent.

Not only was *Plessy vs. The State of Louisiana* a landmark case because it reversed prior legislation that sought to incorporate African Americans into the American fabric, it also accomplished at least two other feats. It provided a legal precedent for the reinstitution of segregation laws in religious, social, and educational institutions for the next five decades.[7] It also strengthened the foundation for Europeans to define people of African descent. The latter remains true today for all Third World people in the Americas whose identities are, in part, determined by the forces that oppress them.

COLOR CASTE AND THE CLUB MOVEMENT

Near the end of the nineteenth and into the twentieth century, there was a proliferation of cultural and self-help groups in African America. Many of these organizations were organized and developed by women. Important for our purposes here, the vast majority of these groups did not segregate its members or audiences based on skin shade or hair texture. Nevertheless, given the relationship that developed during slavery between light skin and privilege, a large percentage of these organizations were headed by well-to-do mulatto individuals—a point to which we shall return momentarily.

Women were particularly active in establishing educational and social institutions for the African American masses. These organizations existed in many parts of the United States, but were most prominent in larger metropolitan areas. Washington, D. C., boasted a number of such clubs including literary societies, art and music clubs as well as benevolent and charitable organizations (Moore 1994). While Mary Church Terrell, first president of the National Association of Colored Women (NACW), has become synonymous with African American women's "club movement" at the turn of the century, there were many other women who labored unselfishly for the advancement of the race.

Helen Appo Cook (1837–1913) is but one example. Cook was the first president of the Colored Women's League and worked arduously to improve the condition of African American women and children. She also served on the Board of Managers for the National Association for the Relief of Destitute Colored Women and Children (NARDCWC) in the 1890s. Cook, like Terrell, was a mulatto aristocrat of color who, along with Lucy Morten, Charlotte Grimke, Josephine Bruce, and Anna J. Cooper, worked for the social and economic improvement of less privileged African Americans (Smith 1996:137–139).

Betty Cox Francis was also active in NARDCWC and was one of the founding members of the Colored Social Settlement founded in 1902. The objectives of this organization were to:

- design educational activities;
- provide domestic and industrial training;
- promote volunteer service; and
- encourage cooperation and unity among colored people. (Moore 1994:413–414)

These goals were laudable, and with European American support and government cooperation many African Americans enhanced their skills, housing opportunities, and recreational facilities. These accomplishments notwithstanding, the nature of educational and training programs tended to reinforce gender-based roles that were predicated on European American cultural standards. Boys were encouraged to develop into "strong and wholesome men and sober citizens" (414), while girls were taught domestic skills such as sewing and cooking. But this emphasis was not unusual because most of the prominent (and some of the not so prominent) African American women sought to embody Victorian values in their private and organizational lives. Upper-class European Americans took pride in emphasizing gentility and "high culture" and proposed that these virtues distinguished them from the lower echelons of society. Middle-class African American men and women emulated these values and in doing so set themselves apart from other African Americans whom they regarded as more impulsive and lacking in self-restraint. African American women in particular were hindered by the Victorian model because it focused on and reified their domestic roles. Although many leaders in the club movement were independent thinkers and did not see themselves as being relegated to the home, the message that they imparted to the women whom they served emphasized domesticity.

Not coincidentally, most of the leaders of reform organizations headed by women were mulattoes of high socioeconomic class. A cursory look at the photographs in the literature (see, for example, Davis, E. 1996) also attests to the fact that the vast majority of women leaders near the turn of the century were mulatto, quadroon, or octoroon. Indeed, in a few instances it is difficult to discern the race of the women. Although "shadism" did not determine membership eligibility in most cases, race and class played important roles in the political nature of the work these organizations accomplished. On the whole, women's organizations, like men's, were conservative in their political demands and took an assimilationist approach to civil rights efforts.

This political position was in keeping with the times—a generation after slavery—when influential African Americans were not trying to raise the ire of European Americans who ruled the day. In the latter half of the nineteenth century, Booker T. Washington advocated this approach, which endeared him to European Americans in influential positions. Washington was in league with European Americans who had money to fund African American organizations and who had influence to make determinations regarding political positions. If Washington did not give the nod, then those who sought political positions or funding to build or sustain organizations would be out of luck. The African American women's "club movement" was no exception.

In 1881, with the backing of European American funding, Washington founded the Tuskegee Normal and Industrial Institute, in Alabama. Tuskegee was founded on the principles of Hampton Institute in Virginia, which concentrated on teaching domestic and industrial skills to African Americans and Native Americans. This meshed well with Washington's philosophy, which posited that African Americans should focus on industrial and agricultural skills and not disturb the status quo by insisting on political gains and social equality. By now it is well-known that this stance caused a long-standing feud with W. E. B. Du Bois and eventually with other prominent African Americans. But for a long time, Washington controlled African American life through his influence with the powers that be.

When Washington established his National Negro Business League in 1900, he extended his power over African American organizations across the country. So influential was he that President Theodore Roosevelt sought his advice before considering African Americans for various government posts. That "club women" were directly influenced by Washington's hand is exemplified by the fact that his third wife, Margaret Murray Washington, was president of the National Association of Colored Women from 1912 to 1916. Booker T. Washington's influence was augmented through his wife, who subsidized and edited *National Notes*, the NACW literary organ. "Some club women argued that this was why articles critical of Booker T. Washington and his policies never appeared there" (Goggin 1993:1227). Another prominent and elite African American woman who held sway in the organization and who benefited from Washington's influence was Mary Church Terrell.

Terrell was a privileged member of Washington, D. C.'s African American elite. Both of Mary Church's parents were born in slavery, sired by European American fathers. In many of these cases, the children of such unions were given technical and educational opportunities not afforded to other people of African descent. Robert Church, Mary Church's father, was apprenticed to a carpenter by his father. After Church was freed, he bought a saloon in Memphis, Tennessee. He later capitalized from the deaths resulting from the yellow fever epidemic and bought several pieces of real estate that later made him the first African American millionaire in the South. Mary's mother, Louisa Church, a quadroon, was also fortunate in ways that most other African Americans were not. During slavery, her owners taught her to read and write and to speak French. After emancipation, Mrs. Church "opened a 'hair store' where Memphis's wealthiest ladies flocked to buy curls and chignons and to have their hair coiffed for important occasions. The store was so successful that Louisa's earnings paid for the Churches' first home and carriage" (Sterling 1988:121). So Mary Church grew up in a relatively well-off household where most of her playmates were European American (121) and where she enjoyed some of the economic and social privileges of European American society.

This circumstance was augmented with her marriage to Robert Terrell, also a mulatto, in 1891. Robert Terrell graduated from Harvard University with a degree in law. It was Terrell's association and political alignment with Booker T. Washington that led to the former's appointment to a four-year term as judge of the Municipal Court in Washington, D. C.

The Terrell's privileged position, along with that of other Washington elites, made them key figures in the "upliftment" of less fortunate African Americans. This largess notwithstanding, most of them offered their services at a distance from the masses whom they viewed with disdain. Terrell was unequivocal about where her sentiments lay:

In no way could we live up to such sentiment better than by coming into closer touch with the masses of our women. Even though we wish to shun them, if we hold ourselves entirely aloof from them, we cannot escape the consequences of their acts. (Jones, B. 1990:26)

Although Terrell was a leading figure in civil rights and women's rights, she went about her "upliftment" with a paternalistic air, and saw herself as a cut above the masses. She even managed to form hostile relations with other women within the NACW such as Anna Julia Cooper and Ida B. Wells, both of whom, while not poor, were not of the same economic class as the Terrells.[8]

Cooper and Wells were less cautious in their political philosophies because they did not have husbands who were dependent on Booker T. Washington's support to hold their positions. The most powerful women in the NACW, Terrell and Mary Washington, were known to exclude Wells from important meetings because of the latter's political position and outspokenness. According to Hine (1993:846), Wells' "reputation for creating controversy was not a desirable commodity in an organization attempting to unite factions of Black women and to provide a public image of reserved, ladylike leadership." Hines and other scholars also suggest that being ladylike meant embodying a middle-class Victorian ethos. Although Wells was an upright, formidable woman, she did not hesitate to defend herself or her beliefs regardless of the political or social issues involved. I suggest that Terrell's color privilege, her elitist position, and her popularity over other African American leaders were mutually reinforcing.

Very few of the women in leadership positions addressed the issue of color privilege within the African American community. One of the exceptions was Nannie Helen Burroughs (1879–1961). Burroughs was born in Orange, Virginia, in 1879. In 1909 she founded the National Training School for Women and Girls in Washington, D. C. (the school was later named Nannie Helen Burroughs School). Although Burroughs was also a member of the National Association of Colored Women, she did not socialize with the leadership of this organization. As Moore states: "Part of this disinterest may have stemmed in the fact that she had no impressive family background and had darker skin and strong African features, both characteristics that worked to her disadvantage in terms of social status" (1994:411–412). Not coincidentally, Burroughs was one of the few women of her time to openly address color issues. "No race is richer in soul quality and color than the Negro. Some day he will realize it and glorify them. He will popularize black" (Burroughs 1927:301).

Burroughs was not only outspoken about the color schisms within African America; she also advocated for women holding equal power in organizations where they were the workers, but where men enjoyed the accolades. In 1900 Burroughs delivered a historic speech, "How the Sisters are Hindered from Helping," which was a major event in the social dynamics between African American men and women in the early twentieth century. Men held leadership positions in religious (and other) organizations, while women performed most of the day-to-day work in these same institutions. Burroughs speech railed against this imbalance of power within the Baptist church and, in so doing, gave rise to the Women's Convention Auxiliary, the largest African American women's organization of the time. Although she worked tirelessly to organize women politically, African American historiography has not afforded her the same attention bestowed on African American men or women who were mulatto and upper class.

In addition to the Terrells, other African American elites in Washington, D. C., including prominent families such as the Syphaxes, the Wormleys, the Cooks, and the Grimkes—to name a few—used European American high society as a template for their own social organizations, which, by their very nature, excluded the masses of African Americans. Although they fraternized with less privileged African Americans in their work, they were essentially endogamous in matters more social. In the 1880s one such group was the Monday Night Literary Society, whose members included Frederick Douglass, Francis and Charlotte Grimke, Fannie Barrier, Mary Strange, Elizabeth Ensley, and Mary Shadd, all of whom were mulattoes, quadroons, or octoroons and were referred to as the Four Hundred. Many of the women in these elite families were wealthy in their own right, having benefited from the privilege gained by their parents based on their mixed-race status.

Organizations in other parts of the country, some of whose appellations were applied by African Americans outside of their group, included the Black Quakers, Black Brahmins, New York's Café au Lait Society, the Shady Group in Chicago, and the Blue Vein Society of Tennessee (Hill 1952:34). All of these organizations sought to replicate European American social structures and habits within their own ranks.

The position of these individuals in African American women's organizations influenced the trajectory of African American history, historiography, and political progress. As mentioned above, Terrell has been idolized as though she were one of a few women who fought for civil rights, when, in actuality, there were numerous women who preceded and followed her who were just as noteworthy, but who have not received the same recognition. More important, the accomplishments spearheaded by mulatto women were bound to be reformist because they were not likely to disturb the status quo that might have jeopardized their own wealth. This is also true in terms of their struggle for women's rights.

Being educated and privileged women, they could afford to live lives that did not require them to be wholly domestic. Ironically, these are the skills that they promoted for African American lower-class women. The contradiction is an interesting one, at best, if only because class, political ideology, and color were— and remain to a certain degree—key factors in determining which African Americans received a sizable share of the American pie. The largest portion, of course, was reserved for men, first European American men, followed by African American men. Many notable African American men who fought for the end of slavery and for equality of citizenship did not consider African American women worthy of these inalienable rights. A few, but significant, examples will suffice.

Alexander Crummel (1819–1898), an Episcopalian minister and a leading exponent of reparations and repatriation to Africa, organized the American Negro Academy (ANA) in 1897 in Washington. The Academy's objectives were to promote the scholarly works of highly educated African Americans and to promote cultural and educational attainment among youth. "Despite the liberal predilections of the academy's male members [including William Du Bois, S. G. Atkins, L. B. Moore, W. H. Crogman] no women were ever admitted" (Banks

1996:58).[9] This was not for lack of the members' knowledge of prominent women activists because in the struggle for racial equality, they were in close touch with women like Alice Dunbar-Nelson, Nannie Burroughs, and Ida B. Wells, to name a few.

Frederick Douglass, reportedly a staunch advocate of women's rights, is also disappointing regarding the African American women's inclusion in the annals of African American life. Banks (1996:53–54) reports that Monroe Majors asked Douglass if he could suggest names of African American women who should be included in Major's manuscript on famous African American women. Although Douglass was well acquainted with many African American women writers and civil rights leaders of the time, he responded that in "his estimation, no [B]lack woman qualified as 'famous'" (Banks 1996:54). There are numerous other examples throughout the history of African America. This is a sad and ironic state of affairs—African American women have always fought for the rights of African American men and women (sometimes favoring men's rights and privileges over their own) while, in the vast majority of cases, African American men conceptualized freedom and equality only in male terms. Indeed, the conventional wisdom that purports that African American women are too assertive was spawned when women took the lead in fighting for the rights of African Americans as a group. Ida B. Wells' efforts to end lynching in the United States is a glaring example of the resentment felt by African American men who chastised her for being too aggressive in these attempts[10] (Streitmatter 1994:56). Although Wells has gone down in history as being one of the seminal leaders in the quest for freedom in America, her struggles within the African American community are less celebrated than the accomplishments of her male contemporaries.

The status and roles of African American women, then as now, present a perpetual conundrum. African American women have long been the workers and foot soldiers in African American struggles, but have received fewer and less prestigious accolades than their male counterparts. At the same time, women have tended to uphold the sexist status quo by putting their rights as women as secondary to equality for African Americans. This would not be a problem if African American rights was not synonymous with African American men's rights. In addition to women's political marginalization, they are subordinated at personal levels as well.

Many African American women continue to accept domestic roles as primarily theirs. While they dutifully assume this character, men are free to do whatever they choose while women are expected to uphold the virtues of purity and domesticity and quietly acquiesce to the roles of gatekeepers of personal and cultural integrity.

The history of African American relations paints a clear, if dismal, picture of a people divided along class, color, and gender lines. Moreover, gender inequalities were not a wholly American institution but were carried over from the subordinate positions that women held in Africa. These uneven relations continue into the twenty-first century in African America with no end in sight. This historical thread is slightly tempered by the increasing number of African American women who are becoming better educated and therefore more economically independent; however, their roles as chief cooks and bottle washers and supporters of male agendas to the detriment of women's rights has not changed significantly.

NOTES

1. Indentured servants in the United States were essentially of three types. One group traded their labor for a fixed number of years in return for free passage to America. A second group was composed of many poor people in England who were kidnapped off the streets and sold in the United States. A third group consisted of homeless people and prisoners whom England was eager to expunge from its shores. According to Coldham (1992:7), from 1614 to 1775 some 50,000 women, men, and children, people who had been sentenced for crimes in England, were sent to the colonies.

2. When Anglo-Americans took over the territory in 1803 with the Louisiana Purchase, they disarmed the African American militia, but by that time, social miscegenation was sufficiently embedded to safeguard its persistence.

3. Of the sources that address the Brown Fellowship Society, Marina Wikramanayake's A World in Shadow. The Free Black in Antebellum South Carolina is the most comprehensive; see also Bernard Powers, Jr. (1994). Other important sources include: Willard Gatewood (1990), pp. 14–15, 80, 156, 225, 280, 282, 316, 340; Thomas Holt (1977) pp. 17, 65–66, 70; Kelly Miller (1925).

Sources that briefly mention the Society include Sterling Stuckey (1987), pp. 199, 234.

4. Foner (1996:61) indicates that Delarge was the son of a "black tailor and a mother of Haitian ancestry."

5. Some of the ACS members included Francis Scott Key, author of the "Star Spangled Banner," Henry Clay, senator (KY), and Bushrod Washington, a judge and a relative of George Washington.

6. Works that add to the historiography of the Blue Vein Society include: Kathy Russell, Wilson, and Hall (1992); Adelaide Cromwell (1994), pp. 13, 16–17; Joel Williamson (1990) p. 82; Howard Rabinowitz (1978) p. 249.

Blue Vein or blue veinism is used as a general term to describe upper-class, mixed-race societies in a number of texts including: David Gerber (1976), pp. 129, 327; Willard Gatewood (1990) pp. 153–161, 168, 174, 345.

7. With the Brown v. The Board of Education (1954) decision, which was fifty-eight years following Plessy, the Supreme Court overruled the "separate, but equal" mandate. Even with this latter ruling, die-hard segregationists resisted integration in the ensuing decades.

8. For a more detailed discussion of the class differences of Mary Terrell and Ida B. Wells, see Dorothy Sterling (1988).

9. Although Banks (1996:58) states that "no women were ever admitted" to the American Negro Academy, Harley (1996:194) avers that Anna Julia Cooper "is the only

woman elected to membership. Even if Harley is correct, this exception strengthens the point regarding the exclusion of women from the organization.

10. In addition to her anti-lynching writings in *Free Speech, New York Age,* and other newspapers, Ida B. Wells documented the facts of lynching in *Southern Horrors* (1892) and *A Red Record* (1985). Her autobiography, *Crusade for Justice: The Autobiography of Ida B. Wells,* presents an expanded account of her fight for civil and women's rights.

Chapter 3

Hair and Color Consciousness in African America

At the close of the Civil War, racism did not disappear. Although legal slavery ended in 1865, neither the Emancipation Proclamation nor the Thirteenth Amendment to the U. S. Constitution did much to change the racist ethos that characterized America. Beginning with the Reconstruction era, the Black Codes replaced slave laws and allowed state and vigilante groups to keep African Americans at the bottom tier of the capitalist economy. African Americans continued to work as domestics or farm workers, making barely enough to survive. Given the absence of educational opportunities during slavery, the only thing that the majority had left to sell was their labor, and this at below subsistence wages. To add to their economic predicament, they remained the recipients of European American mob violence, a practice that has continued into the twenty-first century.

The first quarter of the twentieth century was marked by a wave of lynchings in all parts of the United States. Any attempt on the part of African Americans to advance economically or to struggle for their human rights was retarded by legal and extralegal means. Lynching was the most popular form of intimidation used to obstruct African Americans who were successful in business and who dared to speak out for justice. Internecine divisions predicated on caste and class added to the woes of African Americans.

Much of the intellectual debate around color distinctions was taken up by African American newspaper editors who regularly wrote columns condemning the chauvinistic exclusivity that many lighter-skinned people practiced. One such editor was Benjamin Davis, who, in his Atlanta *Independent*, aimed his invectives against politicians, clergy, and educators, including W. E. B. Du Bois. On one occasion, he described light-skinned African Americans in Atlanta as

the artificials, the superficials, the seemers, would-bes, race leaders, posers, wish-I-was-white social sets, [and] educated idlers....(quoted in Gatewood 1990:158)

Most of the "would-bes" in Atlanta attended the First Congregational Church and tried to uphold an unwritten law that promoted exclusive membership. As indicated earlier, mulattoes organized a number of churches so that they would not have to fraternize with darker African Americans. Still in other churches, members were segregated according to color, in much the same way that European Americans organized their congregations.

While mulattoes thought they were superior, other African Americans felt that mulattoes were physically and morally weak. Many Africans Americans also looked down on them, claiming that they were the offspring of low class "White" men. More frequently, they regarded mulattoes disparagingly because they threatened race unity.

The fact that blue-veinism was widespread throughout the United States concerned many African Americans who viewed color consciousness as a vector that separated African Americans at a time when solidarity was most needed. Although pervasive throughout the United States, blue-veinism was most prevalent in Tennessee, Georgia, South Carolina, Louisiana, and Ohio. In most of these states blue-vein organizations went by other appellations, such as the Social Circle in Cleveland, Ohio. According to Gatewood (1990:159):

In possessing a reputation for "blue-vein element," few cities equaled that of Cleveland. Throughout the late nineteenth and early twentieth centuries references to its existence regularly appeared in print. By implication rather than direct assertion, the "blue-vein element" in Cleveland was usually linked to the Social Circle, an old organization that included the Chesnutts, Wilsons, Greens, and other fair-complexioned families who were, for the most part, descendants of free people of color.

John E. Bruce, a journalist whose pen name was Bruce Grit, wrote profusely in African American newspapers across the country about the internal color line. Like many African Americans, he characterized mixed-bloods as "illegitimate progeny of the vicious white men of the South." Other editors, such as Julius F. Taylor, editor of the Chicago *Broad Ax*, and W. Calvin Chase, editor of *The Washington Bee*, condemned blue-vein color-consciousness and their privileged access to political and social prominence. Ironically, while darker-skinned African Americans railed against mulatto behaviors and their sense of superiority, they themselves aspired to acquire the looks and habits of people of European descent.

This was made manifest by African American efforts to straighten their hair and to lighten their skin, and in some cases, even Anglicize their noses and lips. One Azalia Hackley (1916:33–38) provided what might be considered the most profound example of negative views of African features. She proposed that African American girls were unattractive given the shape of their lips, nose, and mouth. Ostensibly their mouths were too large because of excessive grinning and loud laughter. According to Ms. Hackley, "grinning must cease" because it also widened the nose. She averred that the African American nose needed a "hump" which she thought could be obtained by pinching, thinking, and willing the hump.

While Hackley's was among the most bizarre examples of self-degradation and remedies to "fix" what was not broken, it is important to emphasize that her views existed along a continuum of remedies that would "correct" African American features. Beginning in the latter part of the nineteenth century, and continuing in the present, the African American press has played a pivotal role in advancing the idea of the inferior African body.

At the turn of the century, such products as Black Skin Remover, Dr. Read's Magic Face Bleach, Imperial Whitener, Mme. Turner's Mystic Face Bleach, Dr. Fred Palmer's Skin Whitener, and Shure White were among the concoctions that promised a miraculous metamorphosis. In Chillicothe, Ohio, Dr. James H. Herlihy, a self-proclaimed chemist, proposed that his product, Black-No-More [!] would turn African Americans into people of European descent.

Another advertisement in the African American press read:

Colored people, your salvation is at hand. The Negro need no longer be different in color from the white man. [The]greatest discovery of the age [guaranteed to transform] the blackest skin into the purest white without pain, inconvenience or danger. (Quoted in Gatewood 1996:2447)

The skin damage caused by Black-No-More and many other skin lighteners was so severe that in 1905 the U. S. Post Office barred their sale through the mails (2447). An article in the *New York Times* (1905:12), "Didn't Make Negroes White," admonished companies that promoted products purporting to turn

the black man [sic] into a white one. . . . The first to be ruled out is a Dr. Herlihy of Chilcothe, Ohio, and the Rev. Winfield Company of Richmond, Va. Both advertised that they could furnish a prescription for turning colored people into white. The department detectives sent for the stuff, had it analyzed, and found it to be made up of bichloride of mercury, tincture of benzoin, glycerine, and water.

There are a number of firms offering to supply a drug that will take the kinks out of the hair of negroes [sic] and make it as straight and fine as that of the Caucasian. The department is making an investigation of these compounds with a view to throwing them out of the mails.

These legal proscriptions notwithstanding, advertisements for hair straighteners and skin lighteners proliferated in the African American community. While some Africans Americans, then and now, claimed that hair straightening was merely a matter of style, the captions accompanying transformation agents belie this argument.

THE AFRICAN AMERICAN PRESS AND EUROPEAN BEAUTY STANDARDS

The longevity of internalized racism that prompted consumers to buy these products is evidenced by the existence of Dr. Fred Palmer's Skin Whitener, which was still being sold in the 1960s. Despite the popularity of these products, many African Americans waged vigorous campaigns against the use of skin lighteners. Some of these individuals were cosmetologists who warned about the chemical dangers of skin treatments and extolled the natural beauty of dark skin. Nevertheless, light skin and European features held sway since these characteristics recommended what was perceived as the ultimate in personal attractiveness as well as economic and social privilege among people of African descent.

The Washington Bee, established in Washington, D. C., in 1882 by Calvin Chase, was one of the most persistent commentators on the debilitating effects of colorism in the African American community. Although Chase spoke out against racism and the internecine elitism of color-consciousness, his willingness to run ads that upheld the virtues of lighter-skinned, straight-haired people were contradictory, at best. These advertisements, published in the late nineteenth and early twentieth centuries, leave nothing to the imagination (see, for example, Figures 3.1 and 3.2). Recurring exhortations in captions such as "take out [the] kink" and "Would you Like your Face Lighter Colored for Every Important Occasion?" (*The Washington Bee* 1910) clearly assert that dark and kinky were undesirable. Many of these ads promised to cure dandruff and hair fallout as side benefits to making "kinky hair grow long and wavy." Advertisements of this type were published throughout the life of *The Bee*, which lasted for forty years.

If commercial advertisements were not enough, *The Washington Bee* (5 March 1910:43), ran an editorial that proposed that God discriminated against African American women when he gave them kinky hair.

Figure 3.1
The Magic Shampoo Drier and Hair Straightener. *The Washington Bee*, 31 July 1901, vol. 30(8), p. 8.

Figure 3.2
Ford's Hair Pomade. *The Washington Bee,* 7 May 1910, vol. 30(49), p. 8.

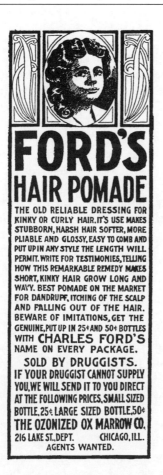

If 'melady' of creamy white, touched with a bit of delicate pink, complexion may blon-dine her tresses, may curl, frizzle and puff her hair, why may not the chocolate brown or saffron hue lady straighten her hair. We say straighten your hair, ladies, beautify your-selves, make those aggravating, reclusive, elusive, shrinking kinks long flowing tresses that may be coiled or curled or puffed to suit Dame Fashion's latest millenary creations, even if it takes every ounce of hair straightening preparation that can be manufactured. ... even God, who discriminated against our women on this hair proposition, knows that straight hair beautifies a woman. Yes, straighten your hair and do it at once.

In one breath Chase condemned the elitism of mulattoes, and in another he published an editorial that essentially vilifies the natural qualities of African American women. In addition to this piece, Chase wrote an article in *The Mes-senger,* another leading African American newspaper of the period, that also encouraged African Americans (especially African American women) to straighten their hair, arguing that it is natural for people to do as the Romans do. This same editor routinely chastised the colorphobia of upper-class African Americans and accused them of having a case of "White fever." Given this position, it is more than ironic that he himself would suggest in unequivocal terms that women shed their African attributes to fit in with "White" society. Other publications of the early twentieth century highlighted light skin (almost white) women with naturally straight or straightened hair.

The Messenger, a socialist publication founded in 1917 by A. Philip Randolph and Chandler Owen, championed equal opportunity in the labor market. Similar to other periodicals of the time that advocated justice and equality, *The Messenger* pasted light-skinned (almost "White") women on the pages of its magazine (see, for example, Figures 3.3 and 3.4) and regularly advocated hair straighteners.

The presence of women on its covers and elsewhere is puzzling in any event because this socialist periodical had nothing to do with women, per se, or women's rights. Even though they claimed to "exalt Negro womanhood," they did anything but this—the majority of women on its pages were so light-skinned that they barely looked like they were African American.

The Colored American Magazine, founded in 1900 and first edited by Walter Wallace, was dedicated to changing the negative images published by its European counterparts. In a historical and self-congratulatory article (Elliott 1901:43–77), the magazine encouraged "those who faint, or would slavishly bend under the weight of a mistaken popular prejudice; and to the inspiration and aid of all our noble men and women, who are fearlessly and successfully vindicating themselves and our people, *The Colored American Magazine* has been and is devoted" (44). Contrary to its ostensible concern with European American representations, the *The Colored American Magazine* presented a very skewed image of African Americans, especially women, routinely promoting light-skinned women with long, straight hair. They also regularly advertised products associated with straight or straightened hair.

The Colored American Magazine was also hypocritical in repudiating the blue-veiners while at the same time accepting ads for skin lighteners and hair straighteners and promoting European images on its covers. They followed the trend in advertising products that promised to "remove black skin" and to "turn the skin of a black or brown person four or five shades lighter" (see Figures 3.5 and 3.6). Even though the goals of *The Colored American Magazine* were to campaign against slavery and encourage support for African Americans in general (Pride and Wilson 1997:31), the publishers failed to make the connection between freedom and cultural integrity.

THE RISE OF ANNIE MALONE AND SARAH WALKER

In the early 1900s, there was a proliferation of hot combs, hair straighteners, and hair pomades. Ostensibly these hair ointments saved women from losing

Figure 3.3
Cover Page. *The Messenger,* May 1924, vol. 6(5).

Figure 3.4
Exalting Negro Womanhood. *The Messenger,* 1924, vol. 6(4), p. 114.

MRS. PHETTA WILSON-CLIFFORD
Washington, D. C.
"Perfect satisfaction"

MISS ETHEL M. ALEXANDER
Cheerful member Washington, D. C., younger set

MRS. SYLVIA WARD-OLDEN
"A most unusual personality"
Washington, D. C.

MISS THELMA HAMILTON
Washington, D. C.
"Those inescapable eyes"

Figure 3.5
Colored Skin Made Lighter. *The Colored American Magazine*, 1908, vol. 14(8), p. 508.

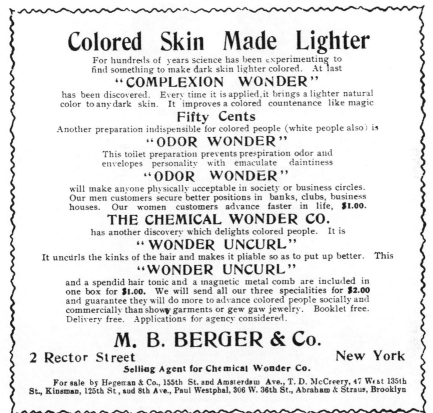

their hair and promoted hair growth. The most well-known entrepreneur in this field in the early twentieth century was Madam C. J. Walker (born Sarah Breedlove). Although popular mythology has it that she invented the straightening comb, she did not. Even though many publications on African American inventions repeat the myth, a biography by Walker's great-great-granddaughter, A'Lelia Perry Bundles,[1] clearly states that she did not (Bundles 2001:20). Moreover, numerous U. S. periodicals ran ads with drawings and photographs of straightening combs at least as early as 1890—fifteen years before Walker even thought about entering the hair care industry. Actually, straightening combs were used throughout ancient European history. In the early twentieth century, a number of Americans adapted new forms of this device. (For a more complete

Figure 3.6
Black Skin Remover. *The Colored American Magazine,* 1902, vol. 5(6), p. 481.

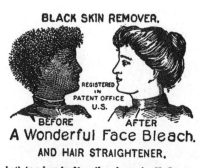

BLACK SKIN REMOVER.

REGISTERED
IN
PATENT OFFICE
U.S.

BEFORE   AFTER

A Wonderful Face Bleach.

AND HAIR STRAIGHTENER.

both in a box for $1, or three boxes for $2. Guaran-
ted to do what we say and to be the "best in the
world." One box is all that is required if used as
directed.

A WONDERFUL FACE BLEACH.

A PEACH-LIKE complexion obtained if used as
directed. Will turn the skin of a black or brown
person four or five shades lighter, and a mulatto
person perfectly white. In forty-eight hours a shade
or two will be noticeable. It does not turn the
skin in spots but bleaches out white, the skin re-
maining beautiful without continual use. Will
remove wrinkles, freckles, dark spots, pimples or
bumps or black heads, making the skin very soft
and smooth. Small pox pits, tan, liver spots removed without harm to the skin. When you get
the color you wish, stop using the preparation.

THE HAIR STRAIGHTENER.

that goes in every one dollar box is enough to
make anyone's hair grow long and straight, and
keeps it from falling out. Highly perfumed and
makes the hair soft and easy to comb. Many
of our customers say one of our dollar boxes is
worth ten dollars, yet we sell it for one dollar a
box. THE NO-SMELL thrown in free.

Any person sending us one dollar in a letter or
Post-Office money order, express money order or
registered letter, we will send it through the mail
postage prepaid; or if you want it sent C. O. D.,
it will come by express, 25c. extra.

In any case where it fails to do what we claim,
we will return the money or send a box free of
charge. Packed so that no one will know con-
tents except receiver.

CRANE AND CO.,
122 west Broad Street,
RICHMOND, VA.

history of the development of hair products, hot combs, and wave machines, see
Appendix J.)

While many African Americans speak Madam C. J. Walker's name with
pride, little is known about Annie Turnbo Malone, a pioneer who preceded
Walker in the hair care business. Annie Turnbo (August 9, 1869–May 10, 1957)
started the Poro Company, a hairdressing business, in 1902 in St. Louis, Missouri, and hired Sarah Breedlove McWilliams (later to become Madam C. J.
Walker) as one of her agents.

Turnbo was born in Metropolis, Illinois, in 1869 and attended high school in
Peoria. Later in her life, based on her success in the hair care industry, she re-

ceived honorary degrees from Kittrell College and Western College. In the late 1890s, Turnbo "began working with chemicals in an effort to find a better method than the [application of] oils, soaps, and goose fat" (Lommel 1993:105) that African American women used in attempts to straighten their hair. In Lovejoy, Illinois, Turnbo finally came up with a solution that would straighten hair and "grow replacement locks. She is said by some to be the first to develop and patent a hot pressing iron and comb for straightening hair" (108). In 1902 she relocated her business to 2223 Market Street in St. Louis, Missouri, where she and her assistants sold her "Wonderful Hair Grower" (a name that Sarah, then Walker, would later appropriate for her own hair cream) from door to door (Friedman 1996:1685). Friedman also suggests that Turnbo "invented and sold a hot pressing-iron as well as several lotions and creams, one for restoring lost hair."

In 1917 Annie Malone[2] turned her business into Poro College, a beauty school located in St. Louis, Missouri. From its inception until the mid-1920s, Poro College became a social center that housed other African American organizations such as the National Negro Business League. Malone's business enjoyed tremendous success, especially from 1917 through the 1920s, as a result of thousands of agents who promoted her products around the country. Turnbo became a multimillionaire, but her business experienced a rapid decline when she and her husband divorced and he attempted to gain control of the business. The bitter dispute ended with Malone paying $200,000 to her husband. Soon after this debacle, she relocated her business to Chicago, Illinois, but her problems followed her there due to her refusal to pay excise taxes. The government seized her business and sold it to pay the taxes. According to Lommel (1993:113), she "died with only a hundred thousand dollars, where once she was worth a reported fourteen million."

In her heyday, Malone gave liberally to a number of African American institutions including the Howard University Medical School Fund, Tuskegee University, and the St. Louis YMCA. The Annie Malone Crisis Center and the Annie Malone Children and Family Service Center in St. Louis are named in honor of her contributions to African American life. Although Malone did not receive the acclaim that was afforded Walker, she was a trailblazer in the African American hair care industry and deserves credit as the forerunner and mentor of Sarah McWilliams.

Sarah Breedlove was born in 1867 in Delta, Louisiana, the daughter of former slaves. Orphaned at the age of six, she was compelled to make a living picking cotton and washing clothes. After the death of her parents, she moved to Mississippi to live with her sister and brother-in-law. In 1882, at the age of fourteen, she married Moses McWilliams only to escape the abuses of her brother-in-law. Moses was killed four years later, leaving her to raise their two-year-old daughter, Lelia (1885–1931), on her own.

To enhance her opportunities for employment, McWilliams left Vicksburg, Mississippi, in 1887 and headed for St. Louis, Missouri, where she found work as a cook and a laundress. She was illiterate, but understood the value of education.

From her meager earnings she sent Lelia to school and paid her daughter's way through Knoxville College, a private school for African Americans in Knoxville, Tennessee. It was in St. Louis that Annie Turnbo hired McWilliams as a sales agent for the Poro Company. Bundles (2001:65) suggests that McWilliams was "one of Pope-Turnbo's earliest sales agents, probably joining her sometime during 1903" (Bundles 2001:65). Other sources suggest that she started working for Turnbo as early as 1900.

McWilliams was one of Turnbo's employees who not only sold Turnbo's products, but used many of Turnbo's and other hair products on the market as a basis to form her own product line. According to Walker's great-great-granddaughter, A'Lelia Bundles, Sarah McWilliams claimed that she came up with her hair restoring ointment through a dream. Nevertheless, historical accounts of Malone and McWilliams clearly indicate that she was inspired by, and adapted ideas and practices from, Annie Turnbo Pope Malone. Some of the ideas and practices that McWilliams borrowed from Turnbo include naming one of her first hair care products the same name that Turnbo had coined—Wonderful Hair Grower; selling products door to door; and giving free hair treatments to prospective customers. Turnbo also emphasized the importance of self-development and character building—tenets that Sarah Walker adopted as part of her philosophy.

Although hair straightening was, and remains, a practice that demeans the natural physical characteristics of African people, a separate issue, in their time as now, is, to whom does the credit go for being the first to develop hair ointments best suited for healthy African hair—Malone or Walker? The fact is that a number of European and African American individuals and companies were developing hair products for African American women. In that light, I contend that it was disingenuous for Walker to suggest that she concocted a unique formula from a dream as if there were no predecessors or contemporaries from whom she developed her ideas. Turnbo, among others, had a definite influence and impact on her methods and her products.

When Sarah McWilliams Davis arrived in Denver in 1905 with the anticipation of developing her own hair product line, she was still under the employ of Annie Turnbo Pope, and, indeed, used the Poro name, along with her own, in newspaper advertisements to make herself known to the public—and known she was. Unlike Turnbo Pope Malone, who was limited by her husband's intrusions, Walker would not be stopped.

Walker's unswerving tenacity precluded anything or anyone from curtailing her climb to the top. There are numerous works on Madame C. J. Walker (Bundles 1991; Due 2000), so I need not repeat all of the details of her life here; however, a brief summary of how she came to be a millionaire is instructive.

It was in St. Louis that Sarah McWilliams Davis[3] met Charles Joseph (C. J.) Walker, a newsman who sold advertising for local African American newspapers. After Davis moved to Denver in 1905, still working for the Poro Company, she married C. J. in 1906. C. J. was very instrumental in helping Sarah promote Turnbo's and later Madam C. J.'s own hair care products. It was during Sarah Walker's early years in Denver that she cut off relations with Annie Turnbo Malone and began her own product line. She immediately began promoting herself as Madam C. J. Walker.

Walker set up beautician schools around the country and established factories for the production of her products. Her products and her fame spread even further after she established a chain of beauty parlors throughout the African Diaspora, including the Caribbean and South America. In addition to Walker's popularity as a hair culturist, she was also a philanthropist who generously contributed to a number of African American causes, including the anti-lynching campaigns of the early twentieth century.

In 1906 she put her daughter, Lelia (who later changed her name to A'Lelia), in charge of the mail order business. Lelia also handled the beauty school in Pittsburgh, Pennsylvania, and the Lelia College in New York. These and other outlets contributed to Walker's rise to become a millionaire.

Walker also strengthened her personal economy by learning how to read and becoming quite a connoisseur of a wide range of classic literature and theater arts. She surrounded herself with well-known figures in political and social arenas and was a generous contributor to a number of African American causes and organizations. But, in spite of her success and popularity, there were segments within the African American community that were categorically against her hair-straightening practices.

Although most women eagerly accepted Walker's products, there were individuals who repudiated her attempts to superimpose a European American image on African American women. At a national meeting of the National Federation of Afro-American Women, one of the contentious issues, along with the negative depiction of African American women by the European American press, was hair straightening. Cornelia Bowen, founder of Mt. Meigs School in Alabama, condemned hair-wrapping, a method used by many African American women to dekink their hair. So outraged was Bowen about attempts to mimic European Americans that she and some of her colleagues formed Anti-Hair-Wrapping Clubs. Other dissenting voices—for example, Booker Washington and Nannie Burroughs—were in the minority.

The church was another opposing force. A small but vocal group of clergymen rejected Madam C. J. Walker. They asserted that if God meant for blacks to have straight hair, he would have endowed them with it (Smith 1992:1186). Alas, this was a minority view. The majority of churchgoers, and others, religiously erased the African in their hair. The badge of inferiority had been securely planted, and by the early twentieth century straightened hair became the norm for most African American women.

Walker is considered a hero for playing a major role in this development. Women still reverently utter her name, not only because she became a millionaire, but because of how she got there. Although she acquired her riches from the business of straightening hair, she was intelligent enough not to use slogans in her ads like "kink-out," "straightened hair," or any of the other disparaging captions used by some entrepreneurs of the day. In spite of this conscious effort to camouflage her hair straightening products, they were essentially the same as others being marketed at the time. Moreover, the representations in her advertisements, illustrated in Figures 3.7 through 3.11, mirrored those of other hair care promoters—European features and long straight hair.

These ads, as well as many others not shown here, belie claims that Walker used photos and illustrations depicting typical African American characteristics. Moreover, even though apologists for Walker's hair-straightening promotions claim that she did not promote straightened hair, in *Walker's Text Book of Beauty Culture*, a client, Alice Kelly, is pictured having her hair straightened by Madam C. J. Walker (Bundles 1991:57).

Even though Walker, in my view, should be applauded for her tenacity and business acumen, it is regretful that she, Turnbo, and others, gained their success with products that demeaned the natural texture of African hair. While hair culturalists of the period were answering a widespread demand, there were segments of the population that took pride in their African ancestry.

MARCUS GARVEY—QUINTESSENTIAL "RACE MAN"

Marcus Garvey (1887–1940), originally from Jamaica, played a seminal role in promoting racial pride. Garvey, who established his Universal Negro Improvement Association (UNIA) in New York in 1917, was a strident proponent of racial pride—the quintessential "race man" who adamantly railed against miscegenation:

I believe in a pure black race just as how all self-respecting whites believe in a pure white race, as far as that can be.

 I am conscious of the fact that slavery brought upon us the curse of many colors within the Negro race, but that is no reason why we ourselves should perpetuate the evil; hence instead of encouraging a wholesale bastardy in their race, we feel that we would now set out to create a race type and standard of our own which could not, in the future...be recognized and respected as the true race type. (Garvey 1969:37)

Garvey waged a scathing campaign against light-skinned African Americans. In addition to his feud with W. E. B. Du Bois over the back-to-Africa movement, the other bone of contention centered on the issue of color.

Garvey was a dark-skinned Jamaican of African descent while Du Bois was a mulatto who took great pride in his French Huguenot ancestry. Although the debate between the two leaders began over political strategy, it soon deteriorated into personal squabbles that were expressed in racial terms. Garvey described Du Bois as a "White man Negro" and "a hater of dark people." Ironically, while Du Bois denied that there was a problem of color distinction within African America, at the same time, he referred to Garvey as a "fat, black, ugly

Figure 3.7
Mme. C. J. Walker's Preparations for the Hair. *The Crisis,* 1920, vol. 19(3), p. 160.

THE MESSENGER

Figure 3.8
Glorifying Our Womanhood. *The Messenger*, 1926, vol. 8(1), p. 32.

Figure 3.9
Madam C. J. Walker's Witch Hazel Jelly. *The Crisis,* 1920, vol. 21(2), p. 86.

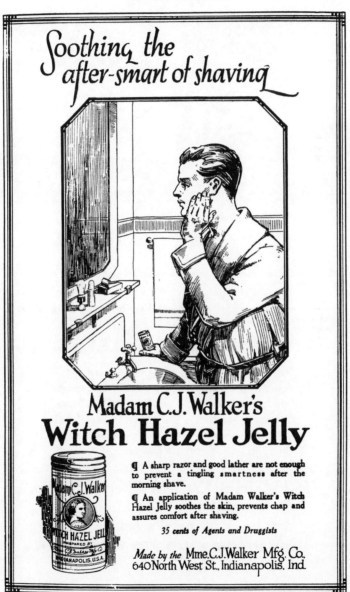

67

Figure 3.10
A Fairy Touch. *The Crisis*, 1922, vol. 24(1), p. 48.

A FAIRY TOUCH

More than a fairy touch is required to obtain and preserve the beauty of youth.

The following superfine preparations have been especially prepared to aid you.

MADAM C. J. WALKER'S

Dental Cream   Cold Cream
Vanishing Cream   Cleansing Cream
Witch Hazel Jelly   Complexion Soap
Antiseptic Soap   Floral Cluster Talc
Superfine Face Powder (*white, rose-flesh, brown*)
Compact Rouge

The Madam C. J. Walker Mfg. Co.
640 North West Street
Indianapolis, Ind.

Makers of Madam C. J. Walker's World Renowned
Hair Preparations

Figure 3.11
Men Prefer Beauty. *The Messenger,* 1927, vol. 9(4), p. 104.

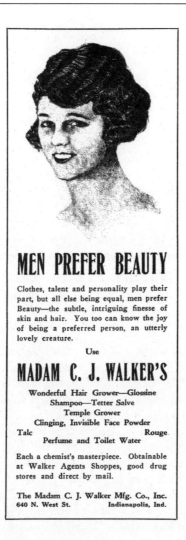

MEN PREFER BEAUTY

Clothes, talent and personality play their part, but all else being equal, men prefer Beauty—the subtle, intriguing finesse of skin and hair. You too can know the joy of being a preferred person, an utterly lovely creature.

Use

MADAM C. J. WALKER'S

Wonderful Hair Grower—Glossine
Shampoo—Tetter Salve
Temple Grower
Clinging, Invisible Face Powder
Talc   Rouge
Perfume and Toilet Water

Each a chemist's masterpiece. Obtainable at Walker Agents Shoppes, good drug stores and direct by mail.

The Madam C. J. Walker Mfg. Co., Inc.
640 N. West St.   Indianapolis, Ind.

charlatan." That Du Bois used the term "black" as an insult, yet was known as the "father of pan-Africanism" is a conundrum that has yet to be explored in African American historiography.

Pride in African ancestry was a consistent and pervasive aspect of Garvey's movement for political and cultural self-determination. Unlike many other publishers of African descent, he refused to accept hair-straightening and skin-lightening advertisements in his newspaper, *The Negro World,* and appealed to other African American publications to stop carrying such advertisements.

Apparently, other publishers were more concerned about the dollar return than the inferior image painted of their people. Garvey remained adamant in promoting natural African features:

[God]made no mistake when he made us black with kinky hair.... Now take those kinks out of your mind, instead of out of your hair. (Garvey 1978:29)

Garvey was also keenly aware of the effects of White dolls on the minds of young African American children and thus joined other African Americans in insisting that Black dolls would give children more positive self-images.

Mothers! give your children dolls that look like them to play with and cuddle. They will learn as they grow older to love and care for their own children, and not neglect them. (29)

Garvey also used *The Negro World* to expose racially exclusive clubs such as the Blue Vein Society, the Colonial Club, and the Pink Tea Set. He also named the National Association for the Advancement of Colored People (NAACP) as racially exclusive because it employed predominately light-complexioned or European American people. Although Garvey initially repudiated the practice of miscegenation, he later implored African Americans of all colors to unite,

even those with one drop of African blood.... For long we have been made to believe that the nearer we approach the white man in colour the greater our social standing and privileges.... But now we have reached the point where the entire race must get together, whether we are light, yellow, black...and build up a mighty race.... (110)

By now it is well-known that Garvey spent the major part of his adult life trying to literally and figuratively reconnect diaspora Africans with Africa (Lewis 1988; Martin 1976). Unfortunately, the U. S. government, along with prominent members of the elite African American middle class (including Du Bois), conspired to thwart his plans for repatriation. Eventually Garvey was arrested on alleged mail fraud and deported back to Jamaica.[4]

At the time of Garvey's incarceration in 1922, the Harlem Renaissance was well underway. Poets and other artists were extolling pride in their African origins—a theme that may well have been influenced by Garvey's agenda. The theme of "blackness" pervaded this sociocultural movement and gave expression to pan-African ties that included the struggle for freedom in America. Fortunately, even within a society where most African Americans repudiate their ancestral roots, many diaspora Africans continue the legacy that Garvey encouraged.

CONTEMPORARY COLOR CONSCIOUSNESS

Just as African Americans are taught very early that their hair is "good" or "bad," they are also taught that their worth is directly linked with the color of their skin. The salience of color within diaspora African communities is indicated by the vast lexicon of terms that denote degrees of blackness (Carter

1944:241–245). A person can be considered "red bone" if light skinned or "blue black" if very dark skinned. A longer list of names includes the following:

peaches-n-cream	skillet blond
yellow	light yellow
chocolate	high yella
teasin' brown	brown skin

These and other color appellations are not harmless euphemisms that have no connections with other structural or cultural institutions. On the contrary, they are in keeping with the knowledge that skin color is an asset or a liability in the American caste system.

Light-skinned African Americans continue to enjoy privilege in a color-coded society (Keith and Herring 1991:760–778). A glaring example of this color disparity is evident among African American Congresspeople. Throughout history, most have been either brown-skinned or light-skinned people. Until the 1960s, relatively few have been "dark." Even outside of governmental ranks, lighter-skinned African Americans enjoy educational and economic privilege.

Based on a study conducted by Keith and Herring (1991), skin color remains closely associated with stratification outcomes in education and occupation. A number of other studies (Hall 1995; Hernton 1965; Lerner 1972) as well as observations of mostly light-skinned people in the media show the premium placed on light skin. This is particularly the case with light-skinned women who are given preference over darker women in TV dramas and commercials.

At first glance, the popular saying "the blacker the berry, the sweeter the juice" (Hopkins 1995:231) may appear to adulate dark skin, but in fact, this adage speaks more to the perception that dark-skinned people are somehow "better" sexually. A more common phrase used by African Americans is "she's dark, but she's pretty"—a commentary that underscores the presumed separation of attractiveness and dark skin. While dark skin historically has been considered a negative attribute, there are many sources indicating that the fact of dark skin color can be overcome by naturally straight or curly hair. The fact that dark skin can sometimes be exonerated by straight hair is only one indication of the negative value attached to kinky hair. It is also noteworthy that the proscription against dark skin and kinky hair is more applicable to women than to men. While both African American women and men are viewed by many in sexualized stereotypical terms, African American men are viewed as sexually desirable because of their ostensible sexual prowess. On the other hand, African American women are viewed as sexually promiscuous, a negative characteristic that has been promoted since slavery. This representation does not render them sexually attractive, but rather, lacking in feminine "purity."

Women of African descent are among the most beautiful in the world. This is an obvious fact that European American society has tried to obscure for centuries. Such an admission would run counter to the myth of superior

"White" beauty. In spite of this reality, white women and light-skinned women are more desired (Allen 1982; Davis and Dollard 1964; Walker 1983) and more financially successful (McAdoo 1980; Neal 1988) in part because European Americans are more comfortable in their presence. That the advertising industry also finds the light-skinned or white image more profitable is indicated by the proliferation of these images on television, billboards, magazines, and other print media. Because the public is fed these images when they are very young, dark-skinned African American women are programmed to eschew their own beauty in favor of a lighter version.

NOTES

1. A'Lelia Bundles, author of *On Her Own Ground: The Life and Times of Madam C. J. Walker*, is not a blood relative of Madam Walker. Lelia (later A'Lelia) McWilliams (later called A'Lelia Walker) was Sarah Walker's only child. In October 1912 A'Lelia adopted Fairy Mae Bryand (Mae Walker) as her daughter. A'Lelia never bore any natural children. Mae Walker's daughter was also named Alelia Mae (Perry) and married S. Henry Bundles. The Bundles had three children, among them A'Lelia Perry Bundles, born June 7, 1952. That the name A'Lelia was handed down throughout the generations confuses the nature of blood ties to Sarah Walker, but as A'Lelia Perry Bundles shows in Madam C. J. Walker's family tree, she is not directly related to the late millionaire.

2. Annie Turnbo married a Mr. Pope in 1903. After her divorce from Pope she married Aaron Malone.

3. Sarah Breedlove married John H. Davis around 1903. The marriage was brief. In 1906 she married Charles Joseph Walker, whom she divorced in 1912.

4. Garvey later migrated to England, where he died in 1940 at the young age of fifty-two.

Chapter 4

Hair and Skin Color in Africa and the African Diaspora

CULTURAL HEGEMONY IN AFRICA AND THE DIASPORA

Divisiveness around hair and skin color is not limited to African Americans in the United States. Slavery, racism, and racial miscegenation were replicated in Africa and in all areas of Latin America and the Caribbean. Europeans held power in Africa and over the African Diaspora, and while exploiting political and economic structures, they disparaged the African body in physical and ideological terms. Africans on the continent and in the diaspora responded by internalizing negative representations of themselves and used all means possible to recreate themselves in a European image.

On my first visit to Africa (Ghana) in 1987, I was surprised to see the numbers of women who straighten their hair. Again, it is mostly women who find it necessary to process their hair; however, this practice is not as prevalent in northern regions where colonial and contemporary European influence was not as great as in Kumasi and regions to the south. Research in other parts of Africa shows that educated African women are more apt to adopt western practices to make themselves worthy as the modern wives of African men whose minds and domestic tastes have been educated by colonial cultural agents.

Although straightened hair is prevalent in Africa and the Caribbean, the degree is less so than in the United States. If the transformation of African hair is indicative of a devaluation of African features, then it would follow that this practice would be less frequent in countries where a larger percentage of people are of African descent. Nevertheless, just as in the United States, other diaspora Africans have also learned to value light skin and processed hair.

Danticat (1995:124), an African Haitian, explains that when she was growing up, she learned that a person's skin color programmed

one's lot in life and, often, [determined] who is considered beautiful—and who is not. . . .
If a dark-skinned woman linked up with a coveted light-skinned man, they would discuss how the unlikely match had taken place.

Danticat's observations encapsulate the historic divide between light–rich
and dark–poor in Haiti. Colorism in Haiti is an especially interesting, albeit
tragic, example of internalized racism because Haitians were the only people of
African descent to successfully carry out a slave revolt against the French in
1804. The tragedy lies in the fact that the mulattoes who assumed power ruth-
lessly maintained a caste society with Africans at the bottom of the socioeconomic pyramid.

Although class is the overriding factor that divides contemporary
Haitians, the correlation between class and color is striking. Economic and
political elites dissociate themselves from the poor masses while exploiting
them economically and psychologically. According to a 1993 United Nations
report, approximately seventy-five percent of Haitians live in absolute
poverty. Life expectancy is fifty-five years and the infant mortality rate is
130 per 1000 births. Reminiscent of Fanon's Manichean world, Fatton
(1997:137) posits the elites and the masses in two separate but interdepen-
dent worlds:

The first world, comprising the wealthy, French-speaking, and cosmopolitan minority,
displays an utter disdain for the masses and sees politics as a zero–sum game. Most mulatto or light-skinned individuals belong to this world. It is antidemocratic and completely excludes the second world from its privileges. The second world comprises *le
peuple* and represents the vast majority of the population. The destitution of this second
world is pervasive. . . . Haitians refer to people of the second world as *san non*, those who
"have no name."

Given the stigma attached to being African, mulattoes go through great
pains to deny any trace of African heritage. At the same time, people of African
descent in the Dominican Republic who occupy the other half of the island
work just as hard to distinguish themselves from the Africans in Haiti by calling themselves "White."

The attention to skin color, along with hair texture, is nowhere more prominent than in Brazil. Brazil offers an interesting case if only because it has the
largest population of people of African descent in the African Diaspora. In
addition, Brazilians are the most vociferous in claiming the absence of racial
discrimination in their country. But at the same time, the degree of African ancestry is positively correlated with the degree of poverty, with Afro-Brazilians
occupying the lowest economic positions. Even though many dark-skinned
Brazilians have progressed economically, the legacy of slavery and persistent
discrimination imposes systemic barriers that impede their advancement on
any grand scale.

Of course, slavery in Brazil was the forerunner of modern-day disparities. So
entrenched was slavocracy in this region that Africans did not obtain their free-

dom from the Portuguese until 1888, twenty-three years after emancipation in the United States. Given the badge of slavery,

it is not surprising... to find that the relatively unmixed [B]lacks are still concentrated in the low-pay, low-status employments [sic] and that they gradually disappear as one ascends the occupation scale, until in the upper levels they are seldom to be found. (Pierson 1942:177)

At the dawn of the twenty-first century these disparities persist. Approximately forty-eight percent of Brazilians have some degree of African heritage. According to Brazilian racial taxonomy, to call this segment of the population "Black" would be incorrect. People who are racially unmixed and dark skinned are called Afro-Brazilians (negros or pretos), mixed-race people are pardos (brown) or (mulatos) (light skinned with some African features). Nevertheless, Afro-Brazilians are disproportionately represented among the poor, the poorly educated, and the politically marginalized. Only one percent of the students at the Universidade de Sao Paulo, Brazil's largest university, are Afro-Brazilian or mixed race. It follows that this segment of the population is poorly represented among the middle class and elite professionals. Even given these realities, many Brazilians attempt to uphold the myth of "racial democracy" and claim that there is neither "White" nor "Black," but only Brazilians.

The spawning of a mulatto class also mirrors race relations in the United States. The greater degree of European ancestry, the greater one's life chances. At the cultural level, Brazilians use a long list of names that are organized along a racial taxonomy. Some of these terms are:

Indio preto (Black Indian)	Pretos retintos (black Blacks)
Negro mulato escuro (dark Mulatto Negro)	Cabo Verde (very dark skin,
Preto Negro (Negro Black)	with straight hair)
Negro Preto (Black Negro)	Sarará (Light skin, sandy hair)

This is an adumbrated list that Brazilians employ to distinguish light and dark skin, straight or kinky hair. Although many Brazilians would like to claim that these terms are merely descriptive, there is ample evidence to reject this notion. That "negro" is often used in derogatory ways is one indication that color terms are value-laden. Moreover, many Afro-Brazilians try to eschew their racial identity by simply creating new labels, such as blue, cinnamon, café au lait, and encardido (a Portuguese term for "filthy").

That straight or curly hair are considered positive qualities and kinky hair negative is another belief system that falls in line with values held by people in the United States. Similar as well is dark-skinned people's desire to have lighter skin and straighter hair. In the first half of the twentieth century, cosmetic companies implored Brazilians to eschew their African features—dekinking their hair was a major selling point:

Wooly hair turned into a permanent!

Kinky hair unkinked!

Pomades Indiana, Americana, etc. [Japoneza, Fixa] correct defects no matter what they are!

(*A Trade*, November 30, 1936, quoted in Pierson 1942:228)

Even though contemporary ads may not use the same terminology, cosmetic advertisements focus on a European look—white (or light skin) and straight hair. While preference for these traits is ubiquitous in Latin American countries and the Caribbean, so stark is the whitening process in Brazil that a Sao Paulo judge mandated that twenty-five percent of models used in state government advertising had to be "Black." There is no such mandate in other areas of Latin America or the Caribbean where white or light skin is promoted as the ideal.

The color-coded hierarchy in Jamaica is typical of the region. Afro-Jamaicans occupy the lowest rung on the economic pyramid, with Europeans and mulattoes taking the largest share of valuable resources. This political and economic control resurfaces in cultural expressions and dictates who is desirable and who is not:

Such harmless terms as "bad hair" and "good hair," meaning African kink and European straight respectively, are still being used and one can still hazard the guess that certain mothers will prefer a white Glasgow carpenter to a Jamaican flag-black civil servant, for their daughters. (Nettleford 1973:49)

Although Nettleford wrote about these issues in 1973, my field work in Jamaica and other parts of the Caribbean in the 1980s and 1990s indicates that the positive value placed on "whiteness" persists. If one is not actually white, then one's education, speech patterns, place of residence, and close associates combine to codify one's proximity to the white ideal. One who is adequately whitened in this way might be fortunate enough to "marry up."

RASTAFARI ALTERNATIVES

In *Essence* magazine (1990:40) Audre Lorde tells of her experience traveling to Virgin Gorda (British Caribbean). At the airport, an African Caribbean woman at the Immigration Control Desk told her that she could not fly to her destination because she was wearing dreadlocks. The immigration agent would stamp Lorde's passport and allow her to proceed on her journey only after she declared that her dreadlocks did not mean that she was a Rastafarian. Which she did. Obviously, the officer had been trained to presume that anyone sporting such a hairstyle was a Rastafarian who was therefore suspected of running drugs or being too Black in their political defiance of "the system." This behavior was part of a broader effort to inhibit the inter-island spread of Rastafarians. From the very beginning of their emergence in Jamaica in 1930, Rastafarians have posed a political and cultural threat to the exalted European image revered by so many Jamaicans.

Rastafari began in response to continued English and mulatto domination in Jamaica.[1] Beginning in 1517, Europeans enslaved Africans in Jamaica, exploiting their labor for the production of sugar, bananas, and coffee. Like most slave societies in the African Diaspora, a combination of slave rebellions and beet sugar production in other countries encouraged Europeans to end legal slavery. In its place, Africans continued to work under slave-like conditions—landless and dependent on European largess for survival. Between 1834, when Jamaican slavery officially ended, and 1930, Africans in Jamaica continued to revolt in protest to their political and economic marginalization. These insurrections were summarily squashed—sticks and stones were no match for military gunfire. The internationalization of capital also strengthened the hand of Europeans in Jamaica and forced Africans to supply cheap labor for local and international capital.

Color divisions that existed in the United States were—and are—rife in Jamaica, where wealth was largely concentrated in the hands of Europeans and mulattoes. The latter were unequivocal in their sense of superiority in relationship to Jamaican Africans and in their allegiance to and affinity for mother England. Indeed, all of the Jamaican heads of state, excepting Syrian-born Edward Seaga, who became Prime Minister in 1980, were mulatto up until 1991, when P. J. Patterson was elected. In the early 1930s, Rastafarians responded to mulatto hegemony by declaring themselves African and worshipping Haile Selassie as a "Black" god.

Due to the popularity of reggae music and Bob Marley, most people are familiar with dreadlocks, but many people are unaware of the political foundations of this group. Unlike many people who wear dreadlocks today, early Rastas were making a statement about their connection with Africa and their strict interpretation of the Christian Bible. Their philosophy was also nationalist in that it advocated repatriation to Africa.

Their cultural manners also illustrated a rejection of European standards and, to the extent possible, a return to a natural way of life (Lake 1993); this included letting their hair naturally lock. The resulting long locks of hair, that some profess are never combed, came to be known as dreadlocks.

Although there is some controversy over how Rastafarians first came up with the idea of dreadlocks, it is more clear *why* they adopted this strategy. Rastas themselves posit that they received their directive from the Old Testament where it is written that

They shall not make baldness upon their head, neither shall they shave off the corner of their beard, nor make any cuttings in the flesh. (Leviticus 21:5)

All the days of his vow of separation there shall be no razor come upon his head: until the days be fulfilled, in the which he separateth himself unto the Lord, he shall be holy, he shall let the locks of his head grow long. (Numbers 6:5)

It is true that most Rastafarians interpret the Bible strictly; however, their decision to wear their hair naturally also came from a strong desire to divorce themselves from the majority of Jamaican people who had embraced European standards of acceptability.

Both Rasta men and women wear dreadlocks; nevertheless, as in the rest of the African Diaspora, standards for women and men are different. While Rasta men can choose to cover their hair or not, women are obliged to do so when in public (Lake 1998: 109, 113). As is true in many other societies, women are admonished to cover their heads for the sake of modesty and in order not to attract the attention of men. Christian dogma also plays a key role in this proscription:

Wives submit yourselves unto your husbands, as unto the Lord. For the husband is the head of the wife, even as Christ is the head of the church: and he is the saviour of the body. Therefore as the church is subject unto Christ, so let the wives be to their own husbands in every thing (Ephesians 5: 22–24).

If the woman be not covered, let her be also shorn: but if it be a shame for a woman to be shorn or shaven, let her be covered. For a man indeed ought not to cover his head, forasmuch as he is the image and the glory of God: but the woman is the glory of the man. For the man is not of the woman; but the woman of the man. Neither was the man created for the woman; but the woman for the man (I Corinthians 11:3–9).

Photo courtesy of the author.

Photo courtesy of the author.

Photo courtesy of Omobowale Ayorinde.

Most Rastafarian women accept such passages as gospel and always cover their hair in public and in religious settings. The Rasta woman who covers her dreadlocks when she pleases is different from the masses in that she is usually better educated and economically independent from a male partner (Lake 1994:243).

The double standard regarding head coverings notwithstanding, Rastafarians were once one of the most revolutionary groups in the African Diaspora. Alas, police suppression of the organization in the 1950s and 1960s blunted their aggressive stance and left them only with their cultural expressions of identity. And even these, in some cases, have become commercial paraphernalia that only enhance the experiences of American and other tourists. Accordingly, many Rasta men routinely proposition women of European descent and often catch their prey based on the allure of reggae, *ganja*, and dreadlocks. So common is this practice that "rent-a-Rasta" is an oft-heard phrase in Jamaica. Nevertheless, the spread of reggae music in the past few decades has also popularized dreadlocks in other parts of the African Diaspora.

In the United States, an increasing number of African Americans are locking their hair. As mentioned previously, these dreadlocks do not always mean that the wearers are proud of their African ancestry. But in some cases it does. Many African Americans wear dreadlocks to symbolize the acceptance of their African heritage and to convey their commitment to a pan-African ideology. As discussed earlier, this expression is only the beginning of a broader complex of ideas and actions conducive to promoting self-determination.

NOTE

1. For a thorough treatment of Rastafarian historical and cultural roots, see Barrett (1977).

Chapter 5

The Dekinking of African Hair

Is your hair still political?
Tell me when it starts to burn.

—Audre Lorde

This is a story of rage, shame and rain. Or better yet, of fear, loathing and ignorance. This is the story of my hair—the most disruptive part of my life. As women, we have heard our hair called our crowning glory, but for many African American women it has become a test of will, courage and honesty. (Green 1993:38)

This quotation from an African American woman matches hundreds of others (see for example, Berry 1996; Gibson 1995; Tarpley 1995) that speak to the devaluation of African hair texture and the premium placed on straightened hair. In this chapter I focus on the different ways that African Americans, especially women, process their hair and how these practices emanate from negative perceptions of their naturally kinky hair. Historically, negative attitudes about African hair have paralleled unfavorable attitudes about dark skin color. Although the issues discussed here apply to continental Africans as well as Diaspora Africans, I will concentrate on the latter, with an emphasis on African Americans in North America since most of my data emanates from this population.

In the 1800s African Americans concocted a number of homemade solutions to straighten their hair. Since the early 1900s, they have used a variety of commercial products to dekink their hair that include straightening with a hot comb, applying lye-containing solutions, ghericurling, and wearing extensions to make their hair appear longer. While some scholars (Mercer 1994; Rooks 1996) view these practices as only a matter of style, I suggest, along with other writers (Anokye 1980; Ferrell 1993; hooks 1993:84–97; Kenyatta and Kenyatta 1996; Lorde 1986:62) that African people who straighten or perm their hair exhibit a manifestation of internalized racism. Internalized racism occurs when members of an oppressed group internalize the myths and stereotypes about them. The degradation of physical appearance is not exempt from this process.

African Americans have bought into the idea that thick lips, dark skin, and nappy hair are not beautiful. While I do not suggest a one-to-one correlation in this essay, that is, that African people with natural hair totally embrace their African identity (because many of them do not), I do suggest that the processing of natural hair is one manifestation of people's estrangement from their cultural foundations. Douglas (1970:71) clearly states the connection between bodily and social controls when she writes:

bodily control is an expression of social control. ... There is little prospect of successfully imposing bodily control without the corresponding social forms. And lastly, the same drive that seeks harmoniously to relate the experience of physical and social, must affect ideology.

European ideology was the coup de grâce of their physical usurpation because it convinced Africans that their subjugation was righteous—that they were inferior people in every way, and thus deserved to be treated as less than human. Europeans who invaded Africa knew only too well that in addition to the gun, the word was their most powerful tool. With their foot at our throats they demanded that we totally submit to their control based on the notion that we were heathens and they the saviors who had come to rescue us from ourselves.

Toward these ends, Europeans dismantled African cultural and political systems and, at the same time, ridiculed Africans' physical attributes. Europeans planted these ideas in the minds of Africans with the knowledge that self-hate and the insecurity that comes with it are prime ingredients in staving off rebellion and liberation. Self-hate and competition were, and are, primary forces that prevented Africans from coming together with a level of mutual respect and solidarity that would have galvanized their efforts to overcome their bondage.

It is well-known that African slaves forged rebellions across the nation, but it is also well-known that other slaves aided in their defeat. The latter had accepted their role as servants to those they believed were their natural masters. As the decades passed, many African Americans remain in inferior positions and work as sharecroppers for the descendants of former slave masters. Those who work in other capacities continue to work for slave wages and do little to change their circumstances. Their unwillingness to fight for a qualitative change in their lives, for a more egalitarian society, is predicated on the acceptance of a value system that champions individual gain, competition, and physical beauty. Although sectors of the population have made important strides, significant economic and political disparities between African Americans and European Americans persist (Hacker 1992). I suggest that a more consolidated effort on the part of African Americans—an effort to obtain reparations, to end mob violence, to create our own institutions, would be facilitated if we would come together in larger numbers. We have not done this because our sense of *peoplehood* has been compromised.

This discussion is significant because it points to acceptance of one's African cultural and physical identity as a precursor to other forms of collective activity. Group consciousness is a necessary factor that must precede other forms of collective work of a more political nature (hooks 1995:124–125). And although most Africans in America consider themselves as belonging to the same race, this racial identity has been frayed by centuries of disparagement that has at its center the notion that we were unworthy, unintelligent, and ugly.

Europeans have successfully convinced many of us that they are the paragons of beauty and that only they have the blueprint for creating a cultured society. Conquerors are usually successful at this level of subjugation because the very defeat of the conquered people makes an undeniable statement about their military superiority. Since people of African descent had come to think of themselves as inferior, the logical course of action was to attempt to emulate their masters, even, or maybe especially, in terms of physical features.

To attain the wealth and prestige enjoyed by people of European descent was unlikely for the majority of African Americans. To mimic their mannerisms and transform their bodily characteristics to approximate European varieties was a more visible and more attainable goal.

Throughout the centuries, African Americans have employed a barrage of skin lighteners and hair straighteners to deAfricanize their bodies. They equate European culture with "good" and African culture with "bad" and in doing so factor out African cultural values and practices and highlight a European cosmology of beauty. The data to support this argument derive from decades of observing African Americans, a language that clearly vilifies natural African features, and first-person testimonies that recount struggles to justify wearing natural hair.

Anthropologists have addressed the symbolic meanings of hair treatment in a number of populations (Berg 1951; Hallpike 1969; Derrett 1973; Hershman 1974; Mageo 1994; Williamson 1979). Leach's seminal piece, "Magical Hair" (1958:147–164), addresses the psychological and social meaning of hairdressing in various societies. While Leach agrees with other scholars that hairdressing conveys certain sexual messages, and is symbolic of sexual organs, I suggest that the connection between genital organs and hair is only part of the story. What is most useful for the purposes of this book is Leach's argument regarding the broader symbolic and ritual significance of hair. He suggests that hair is used in many cultures as an element of

public ritual [that can be] interpreted as performance which changes the social state of the performer from sacred to profane or *vice versa*.

Many scholars (Dansby 1980; Greene 1992 and 1993a; Isaacs 1964; Neal and Wilson 1989; Okazawa-Rey, Robinson, and Ward 1987; Russell, Wilson, and Hall 1992) have suggested that in American society it is the European American aesthetic that is held up as sacred and the African aesthetic as profane. African Americans who process their hair participate in a rite of passage to symbolically change their image into one that is more acceptable to European Americans. The rite of passage performed involves a pseudo-transformation of African hair to hair that appears to be European in nature. This process accomplishes what other rites of passages do—they allow people, at least symbolically, to move from one social position to another. In many rites of passage there is something that is removed from the initiates, for example, blood, nails, or hair. In the case of hair straightening among African Americans, the objective is not hair removal, but removal of its African aspect.

In the cultural history of the United States, African bodies—nose, lips, skin color, and hair—were devalued because they were deemed ugly in the eyes of many European Americans (hooks 1995:119–132; Isaacs 1964:72-96). Many African Americans responded to this ideology with attempts to change those aspects of themselves that were susceptible to manipulation. Hair, along with clothes the most manipulable object, has been the primary site of transformation.

That African Americans attempt to communicate social messages through hair fashion is not unusual. Beginning in the 1960s in the United States a large sector of young European American males wore long hair as a way of demonstrating their resistance to mainstream norms in general and the Vietnam war in particular. In the twenty-first century, longhaired men may still represent resistance to social norms. Women with short hair have also become more normative. More recently a sector of the American population, mostly in the younger generation, have taken to dyeing their hair with unconventional colors such as bright yellow, red, green, or blue. The deeper meaning of this practice is not clear to me, but it is safe to say that such behaviors are, in part, attempts to make the wearer stand out. Using the primary colors to dye one's hair has primarily been a European American phenomenon, but more recently more African Americans have adopted this practice.

Leach's argument that ritual acts are magical acts fits well within the everyday ritual practices of African American hair transformation. He contends that anthropological theories suggest that magical acts of ritual "derive their potency from the values of society as a whole" (Leach 1958:161) and that we can only discover what these values are (and whose they are) by observing members of the society in ritual situations. Empirical research as well as testimonies from African Americans in the literature indicate that the values adhered to in hairdressing are European American.

In addition to his theory regarding the sexual symbolism embodied in hair styles, Leach also argues that publicly shared symbols "constitute a form of social communication and exist apart from private complexes and form unconscious motivations associated with these complexes" (Mageo 1994:409). While public symbols are clearly communicative, it is difficult to separate private psychological motives from social mandates. I suggest that our private thoughts and motivations are configured within a framework of social propriety. First-person testimonies from African Americans regarding their decisions to "go natural" or not indicate the dynamic interplay between the psychological and the social.

Despite the fact that people adopt styles to symbolize age, sexuality, marital status, parity, and economic position, some scholars contend that the African American ritual of processing (straightening or perming) their hair is only a matter of style. Mercer (1994) has written the most frequently cited exegesis on this topic. Even though he acknowledges that "whiteness was the measure of true beauty condemning Europe's Other to eternal ugliness" (102) and that African Americans exhibit "psychic inferiorization," he dismisses his own argument when he proceeds to refer to Diaspora African attempts to imitate European Americans as a "process of creolizing stylization" (119). That is, according to Mercer "conked" African American hair worn by men may resemble European American hair, but "inflections and accentuations introduced by artificial means of stylization emphasized *difference* (emphasis in original)" (119). Mercer's attention to inflection and accentuation begs the question as to why African American men cannot distinguish themselves and keep their natural hair texture at the same time. Moreover, he ignores the pervasive negative attitudes toward natural hair that African Americans express in everyday parlance.

Four key factors point to processed African hair and the premium placed on lighter skin as aspects of internalized racism.

1. The notion that African hair that is straight or curly like European hair is good hair and hair that is typically kinky like most African hair is bad hair is pervasive in the African American community. These distinctions are matched by a preference for lighter-skinned African Americans.

2. The preponderance of straightened hair throughout the African American community speaks to an overriding preference for processed over natural hair.

3. Negative reactions to natural hair by European Americans and African Americans indicate that hair is not a neutral issue or only a matter of style, but one replete with declarations of whose definitions of beauty count.

4. The ubiquitous presence of hair issues in African American literature is yet another indication of its centrality in African American society.

I will elaborate on each of these issues, none of which is mutually exclusive, to point to ideological factors that encourage African Americans to process their hair.

"GOOD HAIR"–"BAD HAIR"

The first and most telling feature of hair-processing behavior is the cultural knowledge of "good hair" and "bad hair" among African people everywhere. If one's hair approximates (in terms of curliness or straightness) that of

Europeans, then one is thought to have "good hair." If one's hair is kinky or on the kinky side, one is thought to have "bad hair." This is a commonly held belief among African Americans. Any African American child from the age of three or four knows what these phrases mean in terms of African people (Cleage 1993:40). A related phrase that points to the nonneutral matter of African hair is "going back"—a term that refers to African American hair reverting to its natural condition when the straightening process has worn off. Many African American women with processed hair are reluctant to enter swimming pools or to venture out in the rain for fear that the water will make their hair "go back." "Going back" means going back to African—something few people want their hair to do. Thus, along with the ritualistic practice of hair processing, a language of transformation has been created that devalues African hair. In order to understand how this vocabulary came about, it is necessary to examine the parameters of racial oppression.

CORPORAL MANIFESTATIONS OF RACIAL OPPRESSION

Europeans found it necessary to construct a cultural ideology that deemed people of African descent intellectually and aesthetically inferior. These ideologies coincided with political and economic marginalization of people of African descent and completed the circle of oppression that continues to engulf Africans in the Americas.

The specific parameters of oppression include four main characteristics (Turner, Singleton, and Musick 1984): (1) the oppressed population must be easily identifiable; (2) this population must be perceived as a threat; (3) there must be vast power differentials between the dominant and oppressed populations; and (4) discrimination must be institutionalized in the social and political institutions.

Stevenson (1991–1992:321–338) has labeled this process of political and cultural containment "total war," which he defines as

a complex of predispositions, purposes and procedures in which the central endeavor is to lay waste a people and to destroy their culture in order to undermine the integrity of their existence and appropriate their riches. (321)

Stevenson goes on to assert that the delegitimization of cultural practices was brought about by the promulgation of a language that

created a positive identity that fused humanness with trade, private property, capital accumulation through trade and investment, and progressive development. The counter-identity created the Other, who was wild inchoate and malevolent, able only to produce backwardness.

The fact that Africans were physically different from Europeans facilitated their identification and capture on the continent of Africa. Europeans also used this phenotypical difference to claim that Africans were inferior. Not only did the masses of Europeans come to believe this dogma, but so did the masses of African people who reacted by eschewing their own identities. As Isaacs (1964:72) states:

The flight from blackness and the yearning to be [W]hite have had a major part in shaping the Negro group identity down through the generations. It involved the more or less total acceptance of the [W]hite man's estimate of the [B]lack man [and] the more or less total rejection of self.

To legitimate institutional racism in the Western Hemisphere, there were a number of legal and cultural practices that were set in place. People of African descent were legally defined as less than human and were not afforded the citizenship rights that people of European descent enjoyed. Among other restrictions, legal structures also allowed Europeans to fracture kinship systems, prohibit Africans from looking a person of European descent in the eye, and forbid them from reading, writing, and recording their own history—in effect, the right to develop as a human society.

The language used to describe African Americans was forged into an elaborate system of stereotypes that depicted them as savage, unintelligent, lazy, and promiscuous. Many Africans wore these labels like a cloak. These stereotypes have combined with the process of political and economic oppression to contain African American life for over three hundred years.

The language that culturally marginalized Africans in the Americas was forged into a long list of stereotypes that declared them ugly. Europeans equated thick lips, dark skin, and kinky hair—above all, kinky hair—with savagery (Jordan 1968). The tragedy is that many African Americans have swallowed this myth—hook, line, and sinker. Consequently, they spend inordinate amounts of time and money straightening their hair and lightening their skin to symbolically divorce themselves from their African roots (see also Bond and Cash 1992). This cultural estrangement is key to the success of oppression because it fosters a process of self-denial and self-alienation, which in turn thwarts self-esteem and collective agency—both necessary precursors to the formulation of strategies for self-determination. Moreover, this denial of African identity is part of what it means to be oppressed on a day-to-day level.

That oppressed populations are easily identifiable is particularly apt in our discussion of hair because transformed African hair is meant to give the image of someone other than African. Although it is clear that Diaspora Africans who straighten their hair can still be recognized as African, the symbolic messages that this non-African image sends is powerful. Lutz (1973:358) writes clearly of the manipulability of identity through personal impression management.

A person who has been cast or has cast himself [sic] into the "Negro" role may find that it is more profitable to deny that identity in favor of the more universal one of "human being." The shift from any particular identity to a universal one is tactically wise when the former identity burdens the bearer with stigma.

"Tactically" is a key word here because African Americans are primarily responding to the aesthetic values of the dominant class. Not to do this elicits daily, and mostly negative, responses from both European and African Americans. Because the dominant class has remained in control of education and other institutions that affect African Americans' efforts toward upward mobility, there is a strong impetus to fit into a European American mold. The concern with fitting in with the American mainstream (defined as the European American mainstream) clearly emerges from Ross' interview data (1995).

Ross interviewed and collected surveys from fifty-seven African American female university students. Forty-six, or approximately eighty percent, of the students processed their hair. In response to a survey question, "Why do you straighten your hair?" the following were among the responses.

- Society [or] dominant culture tends to take efforts that are not considered "mainstream" as radical and threatening. In addition, it doesn't mesh with the dominant society's concept of "beauty."

- Because it's not the norm and in this environment, people don't know how to react.

- My employer might not find it professional.

Based on these responses, as well as others in this study, it is clear that these students are aware of the perceptions that some European Americans have about natural hair. Their decision to comply with European American expectations, and their willingness to participate in a ritual process that consumes a great deal of time and money, is indicative of their own lack of cultural integrity (hooks 1995:122).

Although many people contend that the reason African Americans straighten their hair is to allow for more versatility, a review of the literature on African hair fashions (see, for example, Sonuga 1976) and hairdressing during the slave era (Elliot 1948; Sagay 1983; Schapera 1930) clearly demonstrates that natural African hair can be styled in a variety of ways.

PRE-COLONIAL AFRICAN HAIR

Prior to the arrival of Berbers, Phoenicians, Arabs, and Europeans to the shores of Africa, Africans arranged their hair in a multitude of elegant hairdos that remain into the present (Scherz, Scherz, Taapopi, and Otto 1992). African hair configurations were never just a matter of style, but like scarification on African bodies, hairstyles reflected sex, social status and cultural affiliation. In some areas, occupation could also be deduced from hair designs (White and White 1995:49). The kinky texture of African hair lent itself to many elaborate styles (Sagay 1983; Thornton 1992:230). While some African groups used hair extensions or natural chemicals that temporarily changed the texture of their hair, these chemicals and additions were often worn along with natural hair and were used less frequently than styles that maintained all natural African hair.

Among the Mende in Sierra Leone, women wore a number of hair styles.

Great hair is praised as *kpotongo*—literally, "it is much, abundant, plentiful."...
[Women's hair was expected to be] well-groomed; merely to be presentable, a woman's
hair must be clean, oiled, and plaited. For the sake of elegance and sexual appeal, hair
must be shaped into beautiful and complicated styles...disheveled, neglected hair is
anathema to Mende. It signifies insanity. ... Mende culture finds it morally unfitting to
leave the hair unarranged and equates wild hair with wild behavior. (Boone 1986:
184–186)

According to these descriptions of African hair styles, it is clear that natural
hair was not a barrier to versatility.

Various combinations of braids, plaits (often with shells, beads, or strips of material
woven in), shaved areas, and areas cut into different lengths to make patterns adorned
the heads of people, creating a stunning effect. (Thornton 1992:230)

Hair styling was an important issue for a number of African groups (Sagay
1983; Scherz, Scherz, Taapopi, and Otto 1992; White and White 1995; Kinard
1997). Some styles are only worn by adult women who have completed initia-
tion ceremonies indicating their eligibility for marriage. Other styles were de-
signed according to personal preference or as protection from climatic
conditions (Scherz, Scherz, Taapopi, and Otto 1992:18). The variety of traditional hairstyles supports the argument being offered here that African hair design encompasses an infinite number of styles and does not preclude versatility.
    What we know about how Africans treated their hair during the slave era
mostly comes from photographs, slave advertisements, and newspaper accounts
describing runaway slaves. Using these data, White and White (1995:50–51)
describe the variety of styles exhibited by African slaves.

An African American's hair might be closely cropped on the crown but left long elsewhere; it could be tied behind in a queue, frizzed, combed high from the forehead,
plaited, curled on each side of the face, filleted, cut in the form of a circle on the crown,
knotted on top of the head, or worn bushy and long below the ears.

Generally, Africans slaves could groom their hair as they pleased; nevertheless, there were times when "the bodies of African and African American slaves
were surfaces on which were inscribed the signs of inferior status" (White and
White 1995:48). Some slave owners resorted to hair cropping or head shaving
as a form of punishment (Patterson 1982:60–62; White and White 1995:49).
    The literature on African slavery in America describes a wide variety of
styles worn by African slaves (see, for example, Figures 1, 5, 6, 16, and 72 in
Campbell 1991). Because slaves were made to work "from sun up to can't see,"
the only time they had to tend to their hair was on Sundays. Hair care implements were scarce so that Africans were compelled to use a number of instruments to groom their hair. These included cotton and wool cards (implements
used to brush fibers on woolly cloth also called Jim-Crow), a curry comb, and

other "instruments used to remove dead hairs from animals, making their coats smooth and shining" (Morrow 1973:35). In spite of the scarcity of adequate combs, Africans in America maintained many of the styles they were accustomed to in Africa, including plaiting their hair and winding it with strings of cotton. While most Africans maintained the original texture of their hair, some would straighten their hair by applying grease and then covering their heads with a heated cloth. Near the end of the nineteenth century, hair-curling and hair-straightening technology was more available.

THE PREPONDERANCE OF STRAIGHTENED HAIR

The most telling factor that underscores the symbolic meaning of straightened hair is its frequency among the African American population. Observing African American women in many parts of the country, it is safe to say that at least ninety percent of women find it necessary to change the texture of their hair. If hair texture were the neutral issue that some claim, then indeed, Mercer's notion of *creole* would be reflected in a number of different styles incorporating processed and natural hair.

The vast majority of contemporary African Americans, especially women, process their hair. A cursory look around most environments—the workplace, in the street, on television, in movies—reveals the overriding preponderance of African American women who straighten or perm their hair. From my perspective the question is a glaring one—why? And why the preponderance of women compared to men?

Let me say first that there was a time in the late 1950s and early 1960s when a small sector of African American men and boys thought that straightening their hair was a "hip" thing to do. Whether it was the economic expense or the burning sensation created by the lye in "konkaleen" that contributed to a near cessation of this practice is unknown. But it is fair to say that the emphasis on Black Power and pan-Africanism in the 1960s may have convinced most African American men to return to their natural hair texture. Alas, this "racial pride" began to erode beginning in the late 1990s, especially in large, poor urban areas where there is a concentration of African Americans. Even with this resurgence, the number of African American men who engage in hair straightening or ghericurling is considerably less than it is for African American women. To properly embark on the reasons behind this disparity, it is necessary to make a few initial comments about women as a group and then follow this with a discussion of whose standards of beauty count.

Women in all societies are objectified. That is, they are not seen as equal participants or as having equal value to men in normal situations. Rather, most of the time, they are seen as sex objects whose roles are defined by and only in relationship to men. Providing sexual favors and otherwise serving men are seen as their primary or only functions. Given that most women have internalized these roles, they spend an inordinate amount of time "making up" in order to symbolically present themselves as obedient to their prescribed roles.

I suggest that African American women, like European American women, place inordinate and unnecessary emphasis on cosmetic beauty in order to create the feminine figure prescribed for them by cosmetic companies. Moreover, because the images that African American women emulate are European, these superficial transformations would naturally not reflect their African ancestry. Instead, African American women are contained within a carefully constructed mélange of stereotypes that devalues their image.

These stereotypes—Sapphire, Jezebel, Mammy, and the Matriarch—are disabling because they have come to define African American women normatively. African American women who are characterized as ill-tempered and noncompliant are labeled Sapphires (Christian 1985). These roles are often promoted on television (for example, Keenan Ivory Wayans' In Living Color), in movies, music lyrics and popular literature. It is also remarkable that women (or men in drag or blackface) who play these roles are always dark-skinned (hooks 1995:127). African American women who are represented as lascivious and promiscuous are embodied in the Jezebel stereotype (for example, the character played by Grace Jones in Boomerang) depicting a woman who is sexually provocative and "governed entirely by libido" (Zinn and Dill 1994:267). Mammy is another popular African American female stereotype[1] in which women are seen as foot-scraping, ignorant maids and caretakers of European American children.

Another negative description of African American women that is considered truly definitive of their character and role is that of Matriarch—the woman who is bossy and who acts like a man (Wallace 1979:91). This claim is often rationalized by the fact that a disproportionate number of African American women are heads of households and, as such, are obliged to take on the roles and responsibilities ordinarily assumed by both female and male parents with the male as the traditional and legal head of household.

Whether an African American woman is living in a household with a man or not, she is characterized as "too aggressive" and "matriarchal"—a characterization that is both sexist and racist. It is sexist because it assumes that assertiveness, aggressiveness, and outspokenness are male preserves and innate male characteristics. The idea that matriarchy predominates within the African American community also assumes a European American female model that all other women should aspire to. Even though there are many cases in which African American women are subservient to and defer to men, in other arenas they are assertive in their everyday, face-to-face behaviors. This is part of our cultural makeup as an African people. To label this behavior male or matriarchal (which assumes real power[2] that women have never had anywhere) is to presume that only men should be assertive. The pervasiveness of these misrepresentations makes it very difficult for African American women to find positive images of themselves. Thus, in attempts to distance themselves from their natural or cultural origins, many African American women go through innumerable changes, including hair processing, to look other than African. Ways in which African American women are viewed differently from men relative to hair is indicated in the double standard within the Nation of Islam (Black Muslims).

The Nation of Islam (NOI) was one of the first organizations (after Marcus Garvey's UNIA) to promulgate pride in African ancestry. Members of this group were encouraged to wear their hair naturally—to do otherwise would indicate a mark of shame in one's Africanness and portray an attempt to comply with European American aesthetic standards.

In the film *Malcolm X*, Malcolm Little is admonished by his Muslim prison mate for putting lye in his hair in order to resemble the "white man." This was significant because part of Malcolm's transformation from "Detroit Red" to Malcolm X was his estrangement from straightened hair. Although natural hair is the norm for Muslim men, strangely enough, these prescriptions do not apply to Muslim women in the film or in real life. Could it be that because women are already considered inferior that any expression of further subordination is irrelevant? Moving beyond the Nation of Islam, African American men at large hold different standards regarding straightened hair when it comes to women (Cleage 1993:40).

The literature is replete with women's testimonies about African American males who have confronted them or ignored them because of their natural hair. Many men confess that they prefer long hair—and if not long, definitely not natural. Whoopi Goldberg and Cicely Tyson have both been chastised by people in their own communities for wearing naturals and dreads. Ms. Tyson was told that although she is a "gifted actress...her short natural hairstyle was detrimental to the image of Black women" (Russell, Wilson, and Hall 1992:86). Another less well-known African American woman said that she was stopped on the street by a brother whom she did not know who asked her "when in the hell [she] was going to do something with [her] nappy-headed-ass hair" (86). First-person testimonies in the literature also reveal African American men who consider naturals to be positive, but these instances are less frequent than those who profess an affinity for women with processed hair. Many African American men also prefer lighter skinned women with long hair. Just as naturally or artificially curly or straight hair confers an advantage on some African Americans, light skin is used as a salable commodity by both light skin men and women (Russell, Wilson, and Hall 1992:107–123).

Just as mulattoes enjoyed skin privilege during slavery and the postbellum period, light skin continues to be a positive attribute for many African Americans (Graham 2000; Russell, Wilson, and Hall 1992:107–123). According to Spike Lee (Nelson 1990):

Whether black men admit it or not, they feel light-skinned women are more attractive than dark-skinned, and they'd rather see long hair than a short Afro, because that's closer to white women. That comes from being inundated with media from the time you're born that constantly fed you the white woman as the image of beauty. That's both conscious and unconscious. . . . But on the whole, talking to my friends and knowing men, I see that a premium is put on light-skinned sisters with long hair.

Lee is an integral part of the media that upholds light skin as is witnessed in his films. He is joined by other African American producers such as Eddie Murphy and John Singleton who portray light-skinned, long- (straightened) haired women as paragons of beauty. Kathe Sandler's 1992 film, *A Question of Color*, focuses on first-person accounts regarding the devaluation of dark skin and natural hair. In it, an African American man is interviewed and admits that he is attracted to lighter-skinned, long-haired women, averring "I prefer lighter-skinned Black women. Then I'm into the hair thing. I like nice eyes and long hair."

These preferences are ones that are not fortuitous, but ones that are ingrained in African Americans from day one. When given the opportunity to reflect on the questions from the interviewer, this same man had this to say:

These questions kind of peeled off layers. . . . I'd like to come off really as though I didn't have any particular preferences or [that] I didn't make distinctions, but that wouldn't be the truth. I found out in your questioning that . . . I had prejudices. I'd like to think I was one way and I'm finding out now, you know, that this is the other side [of] me.

A dark-skinned woman in the film acknowledges that she has internalized negative images of herself, but that she is experiencing a process of growth. Although she has extensions braided into her hair, she says that

braids are a Black woman's great White hope. . . . I think with this interview today, it's almost like therapy for myself because, you know, you are saying actually that you're ashamed of your hair. You're not just telling yourself, you're telling your friends, you're telling strangers. It's not easy to admit, but if you can admit that, you can come to terms with yourself.

Even though most African American women have bought into the European American beauty myth, others express a desire to cross over. Given the paucity of this practice and the comfort women find in accepting themselves, many of them find it necessary to write about their experiences.

I want to know my hair again, the way I knew it before I knew Sambo and Dick, Buckwheat and Jane, Prissy and Miz Scarlett. Before I knew that my hair could be wrong— the wrong color, the wrong texture, the wrong amount of curl or straight. Before hot combs and thick grease and smelly-burning lye, all guaranteed to transform me, to silken the course, resistant wool that represents me. When will I cherish my hair again, the way my grandmother cherished it . . . with hands carrying centuries-old secrets of adornment and craftswomanship, she plaited it, twisted it, cornrowed it . . . and wove it like fine strands of gold inlaid with semiprecious stones, coral and ivory, telling with my hair the lost–found story of the people she carried inside her? (Caldwell 1995:267)

Cornrowing hair is an integral part of African culture that has been handed down through the generations. Although mostly performed by women, Harris (1991:25) writes a beautiful essay about how he developed friendship and intimacy through styling his daughter's hair.

I felt good knowing that with dedication and imagination I could learn to speak a loving, painless language to my daughter through her thick, healthy hair....Braiding Adenike's hair gave me another, powerfully intimate, way to help my daughter gain confidence in me.

The few women in Ross's (1995) study who wore their hair natural had this to say:

- I like the ease and feel of natural hair. It is so much easier than permed hair.
- My natural is three weeks old. I don't process my hair because I feel better about myself with natural hair.
- Presently, I live in an overwhelmingly white population. I find it exceedingly necessary in an environment such as this to announce my heritage as loudly as I can.
- About 10 months ago I went natural. I've had a perm since I was 7 years old. I never questioned it until I got to college. I don't feel that we have to chemically alter ourselves in order to be beautiful. We are naturally so.

Because parents straighten girls' hair at a very early age, it is fair to say that the act of "going natural" constitutes a counter-ritual in which the initiate reenters her own cultural realm. But even with the increasing number of women who wear their hair natural, European standards predominate.

The value placed on processed hair and light skin is nowhere as strongly exhibited as it is in the African American popular media (Strutton and Lumpkin, 1993). African Americans, especially African American women, in film (including Spike Lee and other African American male directors' films)[3] and the print media almost always wear their hair straightened. These women are also usually very light and only occasionally brown-skinned women (Washington 1988:114). Commercials and much of TV programming are replete with light-skinned women. In the past decade or so, it has been interesting to see anyone other than European Americans on television. At the same time, it is insulting to see predominantly mixed-race women representing African Americans as the whole.

Again, popular sayings within the African American community demonstrate values pertaining to skin color. Throughout the generations, Africans were fond of saying: "If you're white, you're all right. If you're Brown, stick around. If you're Black, get way back." Although African Americans may not verbalize these phrases as frequently as they used to, a review of any one of the successful African American magazines such as *Ebony, Jet, Sisters in Style,* and *Black Hair* underscores that these ideas regarding color hierarchy prevail. Print and electronic media controlled by European Americans add fuel to the caste system in African American society.

European American capitalists have perfected an elaborate advertising system that has created an emphasis on a particular kind of physical beauty that has influenced European and African women. Even though European American women go through tremendous changes to curl, lighten, darken, and otherwise transform their hair, these changes are not of the same magnitude or nature as those performed of African descent. To put it another way, in spite of the few European Americans who attempt to wear cornrows or dreads, European hair looks European. The vast majority has made no effort to Africanize or Asianize their hair. This would follow because European women are held up as paragons of beauty.

In a review of twelve issues of *Essence*,[4] a monthly magazine published by John Johnson, an average of fifteen women per issue were light skinned. An average of two per issue were dark skinned. The overwhelming majority of women in these ads have straightened hair with an average of two women per issue with naturals. *Essence* is one of the most popular magazines targeted to African American women, but it is not alone in highlighting light skin and processed hair.

In some of the older ads, that is, those before the 1960s, skin preparations were explicitly advertised as "skin lighteners." Contemporary ads are less blatant; however, by virtue of the preponderance of lighter-skinned models, cosmetic companies continue to promote light skin as most desirable. Not only do these ads with light-skinned models with straightened hair promote a European aesthetic, but they do so at great economic expense to African Americans, some of whom can ill afford to spend their dollars on hair-straightening products. Nevertheless, African American women play into their objectification by spending millions of dollars per year on cosmetics and hair care products (*Jet* 1986:14). What is disparagingly called the

ethnic hair-care industry, [is] now worth $1 billion a year....Struggling with slow growth, white-owned cosmetics companies have targeted blacks, who tend to spend more than whites on hair care. (Wang and Malone 1986:54)

More recent data corroborate these findings. Hamilton (2001:34) reports that sales in "ethnic cosmetics" was $291 million in 1999, which was an increase of twenty-two percent over 1995 figures. The projection for the year 2004 is $372 million.

Just as interesting—or troubling—is that women of color spend three times more on hair maintenance products than average. African Americans account for thirty percent of the total hair care product sales, a figure that translates into $1.6 million in ethnic hair care sales annually. (34)

As noted previously, Annie Malone and Madam C. J. Walker lent much to the development of African American hair care products in the first quarter of the twentieth century. These and other entrepreneurs found a ready market because "[B]lack women who wanted to straighten and style their hair in the

fashionable coiffures of the day found the process troublesome" (Doyle
1989:24).

Obviously, these "fashionable coiffures" were European designs that African
American women felt obliged to imitate. Toward these ends, many used a hot
flatiron that proved as hazardous as it was awkward. Beginning in 1905,
Madam C. J. Walker sold her products door to door. She soon became so successful that she established a factory to produce her hair pomades, and established hairstyling schools in urban areas across the country.

At the height of M. Walker's success her company employed about three hundred people—most of them [B]lack women. And with an annual payroll of about $200,000 and
business amounting to about $500,000 yearly, by 1917 the company was the largest
[B]lack-owned business in the United States. (25)

Walker's hair care business was one of many owned by African and European Americans that concentrated on the African American market. African
American companies like Soft Sheen Products and Johnson Publishing continue to compete for the African American dollar with European American
companies like Procter & Gamble and Revlon. In the 1980s, European Americans controlled fifty percent of the African American hair care market (Wang
and Malone 1986:54).

While African American hair care businesses are the last bastion of "black-
to-black" consumerism, African Americans are not spending their dollars based
on the racial identity of businesses. In 1986 they spent approximately 7.4 percent of their $200 billion income at African American establishments (54). Ko-
rean merchants constitute another competing group that covets African
American dollars with their corner on the wig (and fingernail) market (Jones
1994:279–281). Indeed, the hair care and cosmetic industry are prime examples
of the lack of control that African Americans have economically and culturally.

In one particular case, a European American company, Shark (owned by
Brian Marks), sued an African American company for using the colors red,
black, and green (African American nationalist colors) and the term "African"
in its product lines (298–300). This was the ultimate insult! The appropriation
of African names and symbols is indicative of the lack of control African Americans have over their cultural capital. This case also underscores the fact that
African American companies, although players within the capitalist system, are
pawns in a game in which European Americans set the standards and make the
rules.

Even though cosmetic companies promote Eurocentric definitions of style
and beauty, sometimes their advertisements attempt to "have their natural and
straighten it too." They accomplish this by dressing women or men in African
garb and using captions that signify "African," "Afrocentricity," or "natural"
while at the same time displaying an African American with straightened hair.
The product being sold is usually a hair cream for straightened hair, a hair
straightener, or relaxer. Witness the following ads:

AD CAPTION

In the name of beauty we damage our hair. ... For our Afrocentric beauty and style ... it's time to get MAX! (*Sisters in Style* 1996:25)

The model in this ad is a very light-skinned African American woman—the common choice in African American magazines—with straightened hair. Presumably, what makes her Afrocentric is the leopard-skin coat falling off of her bare shoulders.

AD CAPTION

The feel.
The look.
The difference.
African Pride puts the secret to beautiful skin right in the palm of your hand. (*Essence* 1996:57)

One of the ingredients listed in this ad for a "moisturizing complexion bar" is "African Shea Butter." But the model in the ad exudes anything but African in her mini, spaghetti-strapped dress and straightened hair. Other products and brand names such as "Black Opal" and "Dark" and "Natural" ("texture enhancer") use Afrocentric symbols while simultaneously promoting a European American look. That girls and young African American women grow up thinking that processed hair is the natural way is not surprising, given that some of these ads are directly targeted to very young children.

Parents (usually mothers) also send a strong message by straigtening their daughters' hair at very young ages—usually well before they start school. The child also learns by observation that kinky is not an option, because in most cases, her mother, other female relatives, her African American teachers, or other members of her community present her with few alternative models. Those who do wear natural hairstyles are the exceptions, and, therefore, are not seen as normative.

The advertising industry adds to these role models by parading women with straightened hair and by carrying ads with products geared toward children's hair straighteners. One of the most widely advertised children's products of this kind are "Motions for Kids," a product that "allows hair to be blown straighter." Another recurring advertisement in African American magazines is "Just for Me," a "no-lye, conditioning, creme relaxer, children's formula" by Pro-Line. The psychological damage done by such ads is revealed by the numbers of young girls who desire straightened or permed hair. Concomitantly, it is not unusual for dark-skin girls to come home wishing they were "White."

A father of two African American girls aptly tells a story of how a combination of television, chiding from other children, and their mother's straightened hair were too much for his daughters to ignore. Early (1992:34) felt powerless to influence his seven- and ten-year-old daughters to revert back to their natural hair. A combination of Shirley Temple movies and a year of "jokes and taunts from both [B]lack and [W]hite children [convinced them that] they wanted to straighten their hair like their mother." A more recent fiasco that underscores how early children learn that kinky hair is undesirable comes from parents' reactions to the book, *Nappy Hair* (Herron 1997).

In November 1998 Ruth Sherman, a twenty-seven-year-old third grade teacher at P. S. 75, read *Nappy Hair* to her students. Most of these students were African American and Hispanic. When one of the parents found pages that Sherman photocopied from the book among her daughter's schoolwork, she incited other parents to protest the reading of the book because it contained the word "nappy." Ms. Sherman was even threatened by irate parents and was demoted to a desk job at the school. She eventually resigned and found a job elsewhere. The irony of the melee was that Sherman was attempting to "teach self-esteem and pride" but some parents took the reading of the book and its illustrations as disparaging and insulting. What is also ironic is that African Americans themselves use the term "nappy" regularly (and disparagingly) within their own households and within communities. Was it that Ms. Sherman is European American? Was it that the drawings, by Joe Cepeda, were, in the opinion of many readers, including myself, uncomplimentary? We may never know. What we do know is that hair issues are very sensitive in the African American community.

That some of the parents of these children reacted so vociferously to the concept of nappy hair is also indicative of how early and how adamantly negative ideas about kinky hair are planted in children's minds. In this connection, a respondent on a Web page that was built around this issue asks a pertinent question: "What's disturbing about this whole controversy is, Why aren't the parents freaking out about what's inside the head? What's going on in terms of educating these kids?" Norris, the author of an article on an ACB News Web site, states that "at P. S. 75, only one percent of the students read at grade level."

My own experience in high schools in Kansas City, Missouri, indicates that children are more concerned about their hair than they are about their ability to earn a decent living as an adult. In the last high school where I taught, there were approximately five hundred girls—all with processed hair.

The psychological damage that results from straightened hair and the premium placed on light skins is damaging enough, but when we consider that attention to these issues also takes away precious time and money that could be better spent exercising and eating more healthfully, the reverberations are endless. This is not a tangential point here, because African American women are the most obese population in the United States. This is significant because obesity is a risk factor for cardiovascular disease, hypertension, and diabetes, from which African Americans suffer at significantly higher rates than any other group in the United States (Braithwaite and Taylor 1992:90–105; hooks 1993:88–89). The mortality rates among African Americans for these chronic diseases is also greater than among European Americans. These data suggest that attention to substantive changes would be more beneficial than creating transformations that are not only cosmetic and superficial, but culturally and racially degrading.

NEGATIVE REPERCUSSIONS FOR WEARING NATURAL HAIR

In spite of the claim that processed hair is a matter of style, the depths that African Americans go to in expressing their disdain for natural African hair belies this notion. In the early 1950s, long before the "Afro" became popular, Dr. Margaret Burroughs, founder of the DuSable Museum of African American History in Chicago, decided to stop straightening her hair (Birmingham 1977:163–169). Burroughs thought that the process was expensive and time consuming and asked herself "why should I go to so much fuss just to make my hair look like white people's hair?" (Birmingham 1977:166). The reactions from her associates and students was anything but neutral. Students left her notes informing her where she could get her hair straightened. Others suggested that the only reason she would do such a thing to her hair was because she had a scalp disease! On her way to give a lecture at an African American university campus, she was booed—all because she decided not to hide who she was. What is also astonishing about this story is that it could be (and is) replicated today, more than fifty years later.

Given the norm of what constitutes "good hair," it is not surprising that there are retributions for countermanding behaviors that go against this norm. Many African American women are recipients of rebuke from friends and family alike if they opt to maintain their natural hair texture (see, for example, Rushing 1988:325–335). A recent study conducted among University of Iowa students (Ross 1995) suggested that pre-1960s attitudes about hair are alive and well near the turn of the century.

In this study, one of the questions was: "Please briefly state why you do or do not process your hair." The answer from those who did straighten their hair was almost always the same: "Because it's easier to manage." This response is one I've heard before from many women and is one that continues to be perplexing because African women who do wear their hair natural state that they find it "very easy to manage since it doesn't fly all over the place and is less expensive to maintain" (1995).

Students (with straightened and natural hair) indicated a variety of negative verbal sanctions if they wore their hair natural or considered doing so. A few of these responses were:

• People would probably think I was lazy or didn't have money to do my hair if they knew me before.

- My father is brainwashed that straight hair is better, but he's one fourth Indian so he expects straight hair.
- I really don't know what people would say, but I think they would be shocked and they would have a different attitude.

These responses clearly reflect women's concerns about the values and opinions of the "dominant culture." What comes out most clearly from the data is that being African is antithetical to being part of the mainstream. As indicated earlier, young African American girls learn these lessons very early in life (Bonner 1991).

While everyone does not respond negatively to natural hair, or terms that describe natural hair, such responses are common. In "The Pain of Living the Lye," Kim Green (1993:38) shares the experience of having to evolve in order to love her hair. The lye in "Living the Lye" refers to the chemical lye that is present in many hair-straightening products targeted to African Americans.

I grew up mad at my hair because it wasn't "pretty" like the swinging manes of the white children who surrounded me ... As a young child I grew through Afros and cornrows. I suffered the grueling embarrassment of being the only Black child in a sea of blondes.
    ... Those were my first days of true rage. And then there remained another concern: rain. Rain has ruined dates, outdoor concerts and good vibes. I'm a slave to rain. It decides whether I go or don't, and if I go, whether I'll stay. These are the thoughts a simple weather forecast sparks.
    ... Then, of course, there were the days when lazy hairstylists or their new assistants would carelessly rinse my head of the devilish lye, and it would leave scars and burns that marred my scalp for weeks, which frantically itched and reminded me of the power and pain of living the lye. I would scratch my head so hard that patches of hair would give up and throw themselves to the ground in silent protest.

Even though this story was published in *Essence*, the emphasis in their advertising is for products that straighten or ghericurl African American hair. Another editorial (Sayers 1995:162) in this same magazine defends the use of weaves since

women of African ancestry have historically been creative with their hair. African women have used shells, colored cloth and other decorations to adorn it. Our ancestors also used wool and fabric to extend their hair. So, yes, our weaves, wigs and extensions have historical legacy.

While it is true that some pre-colonial Africans used different fabrics to extend their hair, this was one style among many and was not the norm (see, for example, Scherz, Scherz, Taapopi, and Otto 1992). Moreover, this practice did not replace the more pervasive one of wearing natural hair without extensions. The contemporary trend among most African American females is to either straighten their hair or to wear extensions in order to give the appearance of long hair. The practice is an interesting one because it constitutes a pseudo-compromise between looking African and looking European.

African American women are also coerced into repudiating African styles because, according to anecdotal evidence, wearing "naturals" is often equated with being unfeminine or lesbian. These accusations are compelling red herrings in a homophobic society within which African Americans may situate themselves at the mast. The sexism and racism embedded in this thinking is evident because it asserts that only European-looking styles are feminine, thus defining femininity in very narrow terms. While long hair may be revered in the African American community, the only qualification is that the long hair not be too African.

The story of Michelle Barskile, a sixteen-year-old high school senior in Garner, North Carolina, who wanted to attend the Howard University Alpha Kappa Alpha (AKA) debutante ball, dreadlocks and all, is one of the more recent testimonials to the repudiation of African hair. Barskile had been growing her dreadlocks since she was in the eighth grade and was quite proud of her accomplishment. Her mother had attended the debutante ball in her day, and Barskile wanted to follow in her footsteps. She bought a $500 gown and joyously anticipated dancing that first dance with her father. Then the bomb was dropped.

She was told by the AKA that she had to pin her dreads on top of her head if she wanted to attend the dance. At first, Barskile relented, but decided she could not go through with it because, according to her, dreads laid on top of her head made her look like one of the TV Simpsons. She was then summarily advised that she could not attend the Alpha Kappa Alpha ball.

Michelle Barskile worked two jobs, was an honor student with a 3.86 grade point average (GPA), and was active in several high school extracurricular activities, including the drama club and track team. In the eyes of AKA, all of this paled in light of her long African textured dreadlocks. This is only one of the more recent episodes exemplifying mental slavery and a continuation of AKA's unwritten policy since their formulation in 1908 at Howard University.

The story goes that AKA was one of those organizations that employed the "brown bag test" as the ultimate test of membership into their group. This litmus test involved a very light brown bag that was held against the applicant's skin. If the applicant was darker than the bag, she was not admitted. A commentary by a user of the Web site "Soul Food Social Commentary" characterized the sorority's mentality aptly in an article titled "A.K.A.—Apathy towards Kolor Association."

You know, I used to wonder how slaves, toiling for free under the hot sun and the overseers' whip, could sing—without irony or sarcasm spirituals like: "Before I'll be a slave I'll be buried in my grave." Now I know. The presence of chains doesn't make you a slave, nor, as the very prim and proper sisters of Alpha Kappa Alpha sorority in Garner have shown, does the absence of chains make you free.

Along with the onslaughts against natural hair within the African American community, European Americans also attempt to constrain choices regarding hairdressing. European American responses to African American hair are not all the same; however, given the vast power differentials between the majority of European Americans compared to African Americans, the former's reactions to African American hair treatment have had a significant influence on hair care behaviors. The African American community is well aware of incidents in which European Americans have requested that African American employees change their natural hairstyles into something more acceptable to European American sensibilities and have fired or attempted to fire them for not doing so. Stories abound about European American reactions to natural African hair as well as formal sanctions imposed on African Americans for choosing to "go natural."

In September 1995, Don Czyzewski, the manager of Wendy's in Richmond, Virginia, asked three African American women, two of them university freshpeople, not to wear braids to work. Czyzewski's rationale was that the braids were "unsanitary" and "prone to bugs and lice" (Cain 1995:8A).

The three young women, who flatly refused to remove the braids, called Czyzewski on his racism, pointing out [that] he had never made a comment about a white employee who had hair down her back that she didn't even pin up.

When the story was reported in the local newspaper, the president of the franchise responded by personally apologizing to the women and reinstating them in their jobs. Even though these women won their battle, other African Americans are engaged in a protracted war for the right to express themselves naturally. This war is part of a larger struggle that renders African American life stressful at cultural and psychological levels. Here is another example.

A restaurant cashier was fired from her job at the Hyatt Hotel in Washington, D. C., for wearing her hair in "tiny braids instead of single strands of hair" (Caldwell 1995:26). "According to Cheryl Tatum, the Hyatt's personnel manager, a woman, said: 'I can't understand why you would want to wear your hair like that anyway. What would our guests think if we allowed you all to wear your hair like that?'" (276). The Hyatt was able to get its way based on "a company policy that prohibited 'extreme and unusual hair'" (268).

Rogers vs. American Airlines (1981) describes a case in which an African American woman who worked for American Airlines was fired based on a policy that prohibits wearing braids in the workplace. Although the plaintiff took her case to court, the court decided in favor of American Airlines, claiming that braided hair was an artifice and not a matter of natural hair styles worn by African-descended people. While the plaintiff tried to explain that braids were a part of her cultural heritage, the court decided, based on Bo Derek's braids, that race was different from characteristics that are "socioculturally associated with a particular race or nationality" (274). In this case, not only was Rogers denied the expression of her African legacy, but the legacy became no legacy at all in the eyes of American law.

Contemporary court decisions are redolent of eighteenth- and nineteenth-century Black Codes that contained African American mobility at very personal levels. In addition to prohibitions that circumscribed political or economic advancement, African Americans were forbidden to carry canes or to wear certain patterns of clothing. Court decisions that determine how African Americans can wear their hair remain part of the superstructure that force African Americans to conform to European American standards.

HAIR IN AFRICAN AMERICAN LITERATURE

The emphasis that African Americans place on hair texture is underscored by its frequent presence in diaspora African literature (Ashe 1995:579–592). In Toni Morrison's *The Bluest Eye*, hair is an important part of Mrs. Breedlove's identity. Her move from a rural town in Kentucky to Lorraine, Ohio, constituted a hellish nightmare. Breedlove loses all touch with her identity to the extent that her domestic work in a European American's house becomes her reality. Off work, Mrs. Breedlove finds solace in the movies and receives vicarious pleasure from Jean Harlow and other European women.

I fixed my hair up like I'd seen hers on a magazine. A part on the side, with one little curl on my forehead. It looked just like her. Well, almost just like. Anyway, I sat in that show with my hair done up that way and had a good time. (Morrison 1970:97–98)

Mrs. Breedlove is forced into this make-believe world as a result of the vicissitudes of poverty, Cholly's (her husband) alienation and violence, and the ridicule she receives from her friends who "were amused by her because she did not straighten her hair" (94). Morrison further reveals how Mrs. Breedlove internalized the perfect images portrayed in the movies:

She was never able, after her education in the movies to look at a face and not assign it some category in the scale of absolute beauty, and the scale was one she absorbed in full from the silver screen. (97)

Morrison goes on to reveal the profound psychological effects that European standards of beauty have on African Americans by describing Pecola's (Mrs. Breedlove's daughter) devastating fall into insanity—an insanity that resulted from her being raped by her father, by the violence within her household, by emotional and psychological violence exacted against her by her mother, and the violent barrage of exalted European American images. The last of these onslaughts gave Pecola what she thought was the only way out of her misery. If only she could be "White," she would be more loved. With nowhere to turn but insane, she splits herself in two and acquires the coveted prize—blue eyes. The story is tragic not only because Pecola has totally lost touch with herself, but because she epitomizes similar processes in the lives of all of the other African Americans in her community.

The Bluest Eye is a masterpiece in keeping with Morrison's inimical style and mastery of metaphor, and one that should have been the impetus for an earlier Nobel Prize. It would have been shocking, though, if *The Bluest Eye* had been recorded as one of the greatest works of the twentieth century because it demonstrated the emotional, psychological and psychic pain that African Americans endure. Few people in the dominant society want to recognize the emotional and psychological legacy of slavery, but in fact, all of us have been scarred at some level.

Maya Angelou (1969:2) provides another example in her autobiography, *I Know Why The Caged Bird Sings*, in which she recounts the self-hatred she felt because she could not become "White"—a longing that many African Americans have experienced to varying degrees.

Wouldn't they be surprised when one day I woke out of my black ugly dream, and my real hair, which was long and blond, would take the place of the kinky mass that Momma wouldn't let me straighten?...Then they would understand why I had never picked up a Southern accent, or spoke the common slang, and why I had to be forced to eat pig's tails and snouts. Because I was really white and because a cruel fairy stepmother...had turned me into a too-big Negro girl, with nappy black hair. (Angelou 1969:2)

The issues of light skin and "good hair" are commonplace in African American literature as evidenced in the autobiography of Gwendolyn Brooks and her novel *Maud Martha* (1953), Marita Golden's 1983 *Migrations of the Heart*, and more recently Aliona Gibson's *Nappy* (1995), among others. African American women writers commonly explore the theme of hair texture and skin color as "markers...used in maintaining systems of oppression" (Collins 1991:90). The high value that most African Americans place on European beauty standards is juxtaposed by a number of writers (for instance, Clifton 1980; Walker 1984) who celebrate their African hair.

Award-winning poet Lucille Clifton sings praises to her Dahomey ancestry in her autobiography, *Generations* (1976). In one of her many books of poetry, *Two-Headed Woman* (1980), she also pays "Homage to My Hair."

> when i feel her jump up and dance
> i hear the music! my God
> i'm talking about my nappy hair!
> she is a challenge to your hand
> Black man,
> she is as tasty on your tongue as good greens
> Black man,
> she can touch your mind
> with her electric fingers and
> the grayer she do get, good God,
> the Blacker she do be!

In the 1960s, many African Americans wore Afros to symbolize their commitment to Black Power. Shortly before this period, Odetta and Miriam Makeba popularized short Afros and started a trend among a small sector of African American women. However, these practices were as remarkable then as now because they ran counter to the overriding habit of hair straightening. The Afro constituted a

bold challenge to a white aesthetic that had long made curly and kinky hair a symbol of inferiority. (White and White 1995:53)

Recently there has been a very slight increase in the numbers of women who wear naturals. In general, it is safe to say that more men maintain the natural texture of their hair than women. At the same time, it is interesting to note that in areas where there are large African American populations such as New York, Philadelphia, and Kansas City (Missouri), there appears to be a resurgence of processed hair among a noticeable number of African American men. This practice also appears to be class and age based: one usually sees young men from lower economic strata with processed hair.

That men too are ashamed of their natural hair is evident from anecdotal evidence. A friend related the following comment from a young African American male when she asked him why he had shaved his hair off. His response was that he "didn't want any of that pubic hair on his head."

Another interesting trend that has increased among African American men in the past ten years or so is the practice of shaving their heads bald. Although many of these men may have taken the lead from Michael Jordan, it is safe to say, given attitudes like the one cited above, that shearing hair down to the scalp is a way of repudiating kinky hair. I also view this as a way of not having to deal with "full-blown" African hair—as a convenient escape.

Other segments of this population have fashioned their hair in ways that are reminiscent of traditional African styles. Ironically, many of these same men prefer women with long, straight hair, and preferably light skin (Drake and Cayton 1962; Neal and Wilson 1989; Washington 1995:40). Nevertheless, in recent years an increasing number of African American males, especially younger men, are wearing naturals ('fros), braids, cornrows, and dreadlocks. These natural hairdos do not necessarily indicate total acceptance of one's Africanness; however, they are, in some cases, indicative of an acceptance of one's existence as a person of African descent.

POSITIVE IMAGES—FROM THE INSIDE OUT

The African American cultural experience is not separate from political and economic issues. The system of economic oppression beginning in slavery brought with it a complex system of stereotypes that in the minds of many European Americans justified the worst holocaust in the history of humankind. Although both African American men and African American women were subject to inhuman characterizations, African American women were also subject to physical rape by European American men. To exonerate this violence, African American women were forced to shoulder the blame and were deemed promiscuous and without moral values (Wallace 1979; White 1985). At the same time, European American women were portrayed as paragons of purity and virtue. These disparities have been perpetuated throughout the centuries, leaving many African American women with

a sense of shame or even guilt, reinforced or cultivated by the preoccupations and perceptions of family members about the relative "goodness" of physical characteristics of White women and the "badness" of those features more characteristic of African American women. (Greene 1994:19)

Fortunately, many sisters (and brothers) no longer take for granted the notion that "White is right" and know better than to believe that "White" is equivalent to virtuousness. Even though the majority of African American women still process their hair and have negative views regarding dark skin (Bond and Cash 1992: 874–888), an increasing number of them are openly discussing hair and skin color, as is evidenced by several Web sites that invite comments on the subject. But, as emphasized throughout this text, we have only just begun. To come together as a people, we must first recognize ourselves as African people. It is difficult to do this if we are pretending to be someone else.

As such, it is up to us, as parents and as scholars (that is, thinkers), to create more positive images to describe African features and to create a vocabulary that celebrates these characteristics. Self-love, from the inside out, must precede all of this. These new ways of seeing could act as a counterpoint to a culture that equates "kinky" with "bad" and "light skin" with "beauty." The revaluation of these beliefs will not occur in a vacuum.

Because beliefs about beauty exist within a racist paradigm, anti-racist struggles must coincide with attitudinal changes that reflect ideas about hair and skin color. At the same time, African American women must begin to interrogate sexist representations promoted by African American men. This is a difficult task when weighed against the threat of being labeled unwomanly, but then, it is also our task to decide what kind of women we want to be. Although our hair does not define our totality, it is one symbol among many that reflects our racial heritage. Hair also encompasses part of our private expression and is symbolic of sexual, cultural, and political identities.

Other scholarly work on hair constitutes a derivative of Leach's analyses and emphasizes the sexual symbols embodied in hair fashions. While sex and sexuality are embedded in hair fashions and ideas about hair, I suggest that one must look at each cultural group in order to decipher the broader implications and meanings of hair. In the case of African Americans, not only are women subject to different rules than men, but race and cultural identity are deeply etched into how people construe meanings of hair and hairstyles. As I have outlined previously, many of these ideas emanate from feelings of inferiority that were imposed beginning with the colonization of Africa. As Fanon (1967: 38–39) writes:

Guilt and inferiority are the usual consequences of this dialectic. The oppressed ... tries to escape these, on the one hand by proclaiming his total and unconditional adoption of the new cultural models, and on the other, by pronouncing an irreversible condemnation of his own cultural style.

Even though the behavioral and linguistic evidence points to processed hair as more than a style, many people within the African American community resist the idea that straightened hair is a symbol of internalized oppression and an attempt to adopt European American ideas of attractiveness. I suggest that this resistance results from the fact that the practice is so pervasive and so normative that it has come to be seen as "normal." Indeed, the ritual dekinking of African hair begins at such an early age that female children accept hair straightening as a natural practice (Rushing 1988:328). The defense of processed hair is embodied in a quote from *Essence* magazine:

If we allow people to control what is *on* our heads, we will allow them to control what is *in* our heads. (Sayers 1995:162)

Unfortunately, mainstream society has already done both.

NOTES

1. Well-known Mammy figures from the silver screen include roles played by Juanita Moore in *Imitation of Life* and Hattie McDaniel in *Gone with the Wind*.
2. Real power here means control over the means of production and major institutions.
3. Even though Spike Lee fashions himself as creating "power" through the media, his films reproduce the Eurocentric images of African Americans, especially women. His films have received popular acclaim in spite of the fact that African American women are devalued, especially dark-skinned women. In *School Daze*, in which Lee pits light-skinned women against dark-skinned women, the former are referred to as "wannabes" and the latter as "jigaboos." Among the many problems with this film is that all we see is a literal song and dance about hair and color and nothing is resolved. Moreover, the dark-skinned women chide their lighter-skinned peers about their processed hair, but many of the darker critics also have straightened hair.
4. The issues reviewed were from January 1995 to December 1995.

Appendices

Mixed Race Names

Father	Mother	Half-Caste
White	Negro	Mulatto
White	Indian	Mestizo
Indian	Negro	Chino
White	Mulatta	Cuarteron (Quadroon)
White	Mestiza	Creole (distinguished from the white only by a pale brown complexion)
White	Chinese	Chino-blanco
White	Cuarterona	Quintero
White	Quintera	White
Negro	N.A. Indian	Zambo or Cariboco
Negro	S.A. Indian	Mameluco
Negro	Mulatta	Zambo-negro or Cbura
Negro	Mestiza	Mulatto-oscuro
Negro	Chinese	Zambo-chino
Negro	Zamba	Zambo-negro (perfectly black)
Negro	Quinterona	Pardo
Indian	Mulatta	Chino-oscuro
Indian	Mestiza	Mestizo-claro (frequently very beautiful)
Indian	China	Chino-cholo
Indian	Zamba	Zamba-claro
Indian	China-cholo	Indian (with short frizzy hair)
Indian	Cuarterona	Mestizo (rather brown)
Indian	Quintera	Mestizo
Mulatto	Zamba	Zambo
Mulatto	Mestiza	Chino (of rather clear complexion)
Mulatto	China	Chino (rather dark)

Source: DePuy, 1881.

APPENDIX B
Percentage Selecting Traits Across Race Labels

Traits n+ (31)	Blacks n = (40)	Negroes n+ (39)	Afro-Americans
Ambitious	15	23.1	24.2
Arrogant	22.5	17.9	9.1
Cruel	10.0	2.6	3.0
Frivolous	17.5	2.6	3.0
Ignorant	17.5	25.6	6.1
Intelligent	25.0	23.1	45.5
Lazy	35.0	28.2	9.1
Loud	55.5	59.9	27.3
Rude	32.5	10.3	3.0
Suave	2.5	10.3	15.2
Talkative	20.0	48.7	51.5

Source: Modified table from Fairchild 1985:50.

APPENDIX C
Names Used by African Americans in U.S. History

Coloreds	Negro-Saxons
Colored People	African Americans
Colored Americans	Africo-Americans
People of Color	*Gens de Couleur*
Ethiopians	Aframericans
Race Men	Race Women
Negro Americans	American Negroes
Brown Men	Africans

Source: Compiled from Isaacs 1964:62 and Stuckey 1987:198–211.

APPENDIX D
African American Organizations Bearing the Term "African"

African Civilization Society (1850s)
Free African Society, Philadelphia (1787)
New York African Marine Fund
New York African Free School
New York African Society of Mutual Relief
Churches
Abyssinia Baptist Church, New York (1800)
African Methodist Episcopal Church, Philadelphia (1816)
African Methodist Jerusalem Church
Free African Baptist Church (1841)
Free African Presbyterian Church, Philadelphia (1907)
St. Thomas African Episcopal Church

Source: Information compiled from various sources, especially Sterling Stuckey (1987) and Sinclair Drake (1967).

APPENDIX E
Original Version of "The Yellow Rose of Texas" (ca. 1836–1837)

There's a yellow rose in Texas
That I am a going to see
No other darky [sic] knows her
No one only me
She cryed [sic] so when I left her
It like to broke my heart
And if I ever find her
We nevermore will part

The author of this song is unknown. It was signed only with the initials H. B. C., written with a quill pen. Even though the song implies that the author was a person of African descent, Turner (1971) suggests that the author may have been a person of European descent pretending to be African American. Historical records indicate that the original handwritten version was composed soon after the Battle of San Jacinto during the administration of Sam Houston. It is preserved as part of the A. Henry Moss Papers in the Archive Collection of the University of Texas at Austin Library.

APPENDIX F
Rendition of "The Yellow Rose of Texas"

The rendition of the "The Yellow Rose of Texas" subsequent to the 1836–1837 version was published in 1858 by Firth, Pond and Company of New York. The writer, again, only used his initials, J. K. The lyrics are only slightly changed in this version, the composer using "darkey" twice in the first stanza. Turner (1971:8) suggests that the composer was the same H. B. C.

There's a yellow rose in Texas
that I am going to see,
No other darkey knows her, no darkey only me;
She cried so when I left her,
It like to broke my heart,
And if I ever find her,
We never more will part.

APPENDIX G
"The Yellow Rose of Texas" Marching Song

According to Turner (1971:8) "The Yellow Rose of Texas" was a popular marching song sung by Confederate soldiers. One Maud Jeannie Fuller Young, whose son was a Confederate soldier in the Texas Brigade, borrowed the

(continued on next page)

APPENDIX G (*continued*)

melody of "The Yellow Rose ... " and called it "Song of the Texas Ranger." This version, released in 1881, replaced "darky" with the word "soldier."

This song is published among "Ballads of the Civil War" in *The Dell Book of Great American Folk Songs*. The author asserts that this version is presented in its original form.

Another version was published in octavo form and copyrighted in 1906. This composition was arranged by William Dressler and encompassed both English and German lyrics. The lyrics more closely resemble the original version, except for the substitution of "fellow" for "darky."

APPENDIX H
Brown Fellowship Society Members, 1790–1869*

Name	Occupation/Political Position
Andrew Ballon	
Henry Bampfield	(founding member)
John P. Barquet	
George Bedon	(founding member)
H. S. Bell	
Thomas S. Bonneau	
Benjamin A. Bosemon	surgeon, Congressman 1868–1873
Benjamin A. Boseman	physician
F. Brooks	
Alexander Brown	
John Brown	
Malcolm Brown	farmer, shoemaker, treasurer BFS, Charleston Board of Aldermen
Moses Brown	
Peter Brown	
Nathaniel Brown	
Harry Bull	carpenter
George Butler	
James Cain	
James Campbell	
William Cattle	(founding member)
Henry Chatters	
William Clark	
John Conyers	
William Cooper	
Charles Corr	
William Deas	
Robert C. DeLarge	barber
John Deledge	

(continued on next page)

Joseph Dereef	merchant, wood factor, real estate (Charleston City)
Richard Dereef	real estate
Peter Desverneys	
William Drayton	
Joseph Drouyard	
Henry Edwards	
[Robert Elliott]**	Congressional representative
James Eustus	
John V. Francis	
John Garden	
George A. Glover	
James Gordon	
John W. Gordon	
Robert Gordon	
John Gough	
Grimke	
William Hall	
R. H. Hampton	
W. Hampton	
James B. Harrison	
James F. Hatt	
James Holland	
Charles Holloway	
James Holloway	
John Mitchell Holloway	carpenter
Richard Holloway	Carpenter Council, 1868
Richard Holman	
Samuel Holman	
Thomas M. Holmes	
Richard Hopton	
[Robb] Houston	
Robert Houston	
Robert Howard	
Benjamin T. Huger	
Carlos Huger	
Francis Brewer Huger	
Joseph P. Humphries	
Thomas Inglis	
H. W. James	
James Johnson	
Abraham Jones	
David Jones	
Jehu Jones	hotelier
Jehu Jones, Jr.	hotelier
Nathan Jones	
Peter Jones	
Benjamin Kinloch	

(continued on next page)

APPENDIX H (*continued*)

Richmond Kinloch	millwright
Jacob Kougley	
Francis Lafond	
John Lee	
William Lee	
Charles Lemar	
John Livingston	
George Logan	
William Lopez	
G. Lucas	
Zephaniah Lyles	
Philip Manuel	
P. H. Marchant	
William Marshall	
James Maxwell	
Thomas Maxwell	
Mazyck	
John McBeth	
William McKinney	
William McKinlay	tailor, landlord
William J. McKinlay	teacher, tailor
A. H. Miller	
J. D. Miller	
Mischeau	
John Mishaw	
James Mitchell	(founding Member)
John Mitchell	
W. S. Montgomery	
Mouzons	
J. B. Mushington	
John Mushington	
William Mushington	
Alexander Noisette	
Phillipe Noisette	
[George Nucus]	
Andrew Ogilvie	
John S. Parker	
William Pinceel	
Edward Pitray	
Benjamin L. Plumeau	
Isaac Prioleau	teacher, laborer, representative (1872–1874; 1876–1877)
Joseph H. Rainey	Congressman
Alonzo J. Ransier	clerk, editor, Congressman
Peter Robertson	
Phillip Saltus	

(continued on next page)

Samuel Saltus	(Founding member)
Joseph Sasportas	butcher
Thaddeus Sasportas	
Joseph Savage	
Richard Savage	
James Scott	
[Castile Selby]	
William W. Seymour	
[Smart Simpson]	
[Robert Smalls]	Congressman
John Henry Smith	
John C. Steedman	
John Studman	
[George Sucas]	
Benjamin Taylor	
B. F. Townsend	
Edward P. Wall	
William Wall	
William Ward	
George Weaver	
Anthony Weston	
Jacob Weston	tailor, teacher
John Weston	
Samuel Weston	
Henry William	
Joseph Williams	
Jonathan Jasper Wright	

Source: Compiled from Brown Fellowship Society Records and BFS Minutes, 1790–1869.

*Although the BFS still exists, the last available official minutes for the organization are dated 1869.

**The historiography is unclear whether individuals in brackets were actually BFS members.

APPENDIX I
Brown Fellowship Society Slave Owners*

Thomas Bonneau	Richard Kinloch
John Brown	John Lee
Malcolm Brown	Charles Lemar
Peter Brown	James Maxwell
William Cooper	Thomas Maxwell
John DeLarge	John McBeth
Robert Carlos DeLarge	John Mishaw
Joseph Dereef	William Mushington
Richard Dereef	William Pinceel
William Drayton	Isaac Prileau
James Harrison	Joseph Rainey
Charles Holloway	Joseph Sasportas
John Holloway	Thaddeus Sasportas

(continued on next page)

APPENDIX I (*continued*)

Richard Holloway	Joseph Savage
Robert Houston	Richard Savage
Joseph Humphries	William Seymour
Thomas Inglis	Anthony Weston
Jehu Jones	Jacob Weston
Jehu Jones, Jr.	Samuel Weston
Benjamin Kinloch	

Source: Compiled from Christopher 1976:97–103; Foner 1996; Holt 1977; Koger 1985.
*The above list may not exhaust members who owned slaves. Wives and other female relatives of
BFS members were also slave owners.

APPENDIX J
Facts about Hairdressing Innovations

- Heated curling irons (or tongs) were used by women and men in ancient Rome, Babylonia, Persia, and Assyria. Various forms of heated irons were used in many parts of Europe.
- Marcel Grateau, a Parisian hairdresser, created the first waving iron in the 1870s. The Marcel wave remained popular for decades and was also incorporated into hairpieces.
- Lyda A. Newman* (New York, New York) invented a hair brush with a detachable unit that consisted of the brush's bristles. (Patent Number 614,335, November 15, 1898.)
- In 1905 Charles Nestle, a Frenchman, invented the first permanent wave machine.
- In 1912 Garrett Morgan* (Kentucky) discovered a hair straightener while trying to create a polish for sewing machine needles. This hair straightener launched Morgan into the hairdressing business for decades after his discovery.
- Walter Sammons* invented a straightening comb that was patented in 1920. The comb had curved teeth and a themometer that was visible in the handle.
- Marjorie Joyner* (Chicago, Illinois) was working for Madam C. J. Walker when she invented a permanent wave machine. She later sold the patent to Walker's company. (Patent Number 1,693,515, November 27, 1928.)
- In the early 1900s Madam C. J. Walker developed a number of hair pomades and skin lotions.
- Solomon Harper, a member of the American Association for the Advancement of Science, invented and patented an electric hair comb in 1930. He went on to patent a series of thermostatically controlled combs and curling irons.

Source: Jenkins 1996; Krapp 1999; Webster 1999.
*African American inventors.

Bibliography

Alba, Richard
    1990   *Ethnic Identity: The Transformation of White America*. New Haven: Yale
            University Press.
Allen, B.
    1982   It Ain't Easy Being Pinky. *Essence* 13(3):67–68, 127–128.
Angelou, Maya
    1969   *I Know Why the Caged Bird Sings*. New York: Bantam.
Anokye, Akua-Adiki
    1980   *African Hairstyles*. New York: Akua-Adiki Anokye.
Ashe, Bertram
    1995   "Why don't he like my hair?" Constructing African-American Standards
            of Beauty in Toni Morrison's *Song of Solomon* and Zora Neale Hurston's
            Their Eyes Were Watching God. *African American Review* 29(4):579–592.
Atlantic Monthly
    1861   Denmark Vesey. Vol. 7(44):728–744.
Azevedo, E. S.
    1980   Anthropological and Cultural Meaning of Family Names in Bagiua, Brazil.
            Current Anthropology 21:360–363.
Banks, William
    1996   *Black Intellectuals: Race and Responsibility in American Life*. New York:
            Norton.
Barrett, Leonard
    1977   *The Rastafarians—Dreadlocks of Jamaica*. Kingston: Sangsters.
Bennett, Lerone Jr.
    1967   What's in a Name? *New York Times Magazine* 23(1):46–48; 50–54.
Berg, Charles
    1951   *The Unconscious Significance of Hair*. London: Allen and Unwin.

Berlin, Ira
    1974   *Slaves Without Masters: The Free Negro in the Antebellum South.*
            New York: Pantheon Books.
Berry, Bertice
    1996   *Bertice, The World According to Me.* New York: Scribner.
Berry, Mary F., and John W. Blassingame
    1982   Black Nationalism. In *Long Memory, The Black Experience in America.*
            New York: Oxford University Press, 333–423.
Billard, Jules B.
    1974   *The World of the American Indian.* Washington, D. C.: The National
            Geographic Society.
Birmingham, Stephen
    1977   *Certain People: America's Black Elite.* Boston: Little, Brown and
            Company.
Bittle, William, and Gilbert Geis
    1964   *The Longest Way Home: Chief Alfred C. Sam's Back-to-Africa
            Movement.* Detroit: Wayne State University Press.
Blassingame, John
    1973   *Black New Orleans, 1860–1880.* Chicago: University of Chicago Press.
Blauner, Robert
    1972   *Racial Oppression in America.* New York: Harper and Row.
Blyden, Edward
    1967   *Christianity, Islam and the Negro Race.* Edinburgh: Oxford University
            Press.
Bond, Selena, and Thomas Cash
    1992   Black Beauty: Skin Color and Body Image Among African-American
            College Women. *Journal of Applied Social Psychology*
            22(11):874–888.
Bonner, Lonnice
    1991   *Good Hair: For Colored Girls Who've Considered Weaves When the
            Chemicals Became Too Ruff.* New York: Crown Trade Paperbacks.
Boone, Sylvia
    1986   *Radiance from the Waters: Ideas of Feminine Beauty in Mende Art.* New
            Haven and London: Yale University Press.
Bowen, J. W. E.
    1960   Who Are We? Africans, Afro-Americans, Colored People, Negroes or
            African Negroes? *Voice of the Negro* 3 (January):30–36.
Braithwaite, Richelle
    1982   *Braid Sculpture. The Art of Combless Hairstyling.* New York: Ruqui,
            I.l.l.
Braithwaite, Ronald, and Sandra Taylor
    1992   *Health Issues in the Black Community.* San Francisco: Jossey-Bass
            Publishers.
Brooks, Gwendolyn
    1953   *Maud Martha.* New York: Harper.
Bundles, A'Lelia Perry
    1991   *Madam C. J. Walker.* New York: Chelsea House Publishers.
    2001   *The Life and Times of Madam C. J. Walker.* New York: Scribner.

Burroughs, Nannie Helen
    1927   With All Thy Getting. *Southern Workman* 56 (July):301.
Cain, Chelsea
    1995   Nikita, Lakeisha and Aleeta—Heroines of a Modern Fairy Tale. *The Daily
           Iowan* 12 October: 8A.
Caldwell, Paulette
    1995   A Hair Piece: Perspectives on the Intersection of Race and Gender. In
           Critical Race Theory: The Cutting Edge. Richard Delgado (ed.).
           Philadelphia: Temple University Press, 267–278.
Campell, Edward Jr., (ed.)
    1991   *Before Freedom Came: African American Life in the Antebellum South*.
           Charlottesville: University Press of Virginia.
Carmichael, Stokely
    1969   Pan-Africanism, Land and Power. *The Black Scholar Journal of Black
           Studies and Research* 1(1):36–43.
Carmichael, Stokely, and Charles Hamilton
    1967   *Black Power. The Politics of Liberation in America*. New York: Vintage
           Books.
Carter, Wilmoth
    1944   Nicknames and Minority Groups. *Phylon* 5(3):241–245.
Carucci, L. M.
    1984   Significance of Change or Change of Significance: A Consideration of
           Marshallese Personal Names. *Ethnology* 23:143–155.
Chamberlain, Houston Stewart
    1899   *The Foundations of the Nineteenth Century*. London: John Lane.
Chesnutt, Charles W.
    1967   *The Wife of His Youth and Other Stories of the Color Line*. United
           Kingdom: The Crescent Press.
    1969   *The House Behind the Cedars*. New York: Macmillan Press.
Christian, Barbara
    1985   *Black Feminist Criticism: Perspectives on Black Women Writers*. New
           York: Pergamon Press.
Christopher, Maurine
    1976   *Black Americans in Congress*. New York: Thomas Y. Crowell.
Chuks-Orji, O.
    1972   *Names from Africa: Their Origin, Meaning, and Pronunciation*. Chicago:
           Johnson.
Churchill, Ward
    1994   Naming Our Destiny: Toward a Destiny of American Indian Liberation. In
           Indians Are Us? Culture and Genocide in Native North America. Ward
           Churchill (ed.) Monroe, Maine: Common Courage Press.
Clark, Kenneth
    1965   *Dark Ghetto*. New York: Harper and Row.
Clarke, John H.
    1986   Lecture delivered at Africana Studies and Research Center. Cornell
           University, Ithaca, New York.
Cleage, Pearl
    1993   Hairpeace. *African American Review* 27:37–41.

Clifton, Lucille
    1976   *Generations*. New York: Random House.
    1980   *Two-Headed Woman*. Amherst: University of Massachusetts.
Coldham, Peter
    1992   *Emigrants in Chains: A Social History of Forced Emigration to the
            Americas of Felons, Destitute Children, Political and Religious
            Non-Conformists, Vagabonds, Beggars and Other Undesirables,
            1607–1776*. Baltimore: Genealogical Publishing Company.
Collins, Patricia Hill
    1991   *Black Feminist Thought: Knowledge, Consciousness, and the Politics of
            Empowerment*. London: Routledge.
Conniff, Michael
    1994   *Africans in the Americas: A History of the Black Diaspora*. New York: St.
            Martin's.
Cooper, Wendy
    1972   *Hair: Sex Society and Symbolism*. New York: Stein and Day
            Publishers.
Cortes, C. E.
    1980   Review of *Listen Chicano! An Informal History of the Mexican
            American*. Manuel A. Machado, Jr. *Hispanic Journal of Behavioral
            Sciences* 2:303–307.
Cromwell, Adelaide
    1994   *The Other Brahmins: Boston's Black Upper Class 1750–1950*. Fayetteville:
            University of Arkansas Press.
Curry, Leonard
    1981   *The Free Black in Urban America, 1800–1850: The Shadow of the Dream*.
            Chicago: University of Chicago Press.
Curtin, Phillip
    1964   *The Image of Africa: British Ideas and Action, 1780–1850*. Madison:
            University of Wisconsin Press.
Dansby, Pearl Gore
    1978   Black Pride in the Seventies: Fact or Fantasy? In *Black Psychology*.
            Reginald L. Jones (ed.). New York: Harper and Row, 71–80.
Danticat, Edwidge
    1995   Local Color. *Allure* 139(September):124.
Davis, Allison, and John Dollard
    1964   *Children of Bondage*. New York: Harper.
Davis, Elizabeth
    1996   *Lifting as They Climb*. New York: G. K. Hall.
De Gobineau, Arthur
    1967   (1915). *The Inequality of Human Races*. New York: Howard Fertig.
Delgado, Richard
    1995   Words That Wound: A Tort Action for Racial Insults, Epithets and Name-
            Calling. In *Critical Race Theory: The Cutting Edge*. Richard Delgado (ed.).
            Philadelphia: Temple University Press, 157–159.
DeMallie, Raymond J., and Alfonso Oritz, eds.
    1994   *North American Indian Anthropology: Essays on Society and Culture*.
            Oklahoma: University of Oklahoma Press.

DePuy, William
    1881   *The People's Cyclopedia of Universal Knowledge with Numerous*
            Appendixes for References in All Departments of Industrial Life: The
            Whole Brought Down to the Year 1881. New York: Phillips and Hunt.
Derrett, J. Duncan
    1973   Religious Hair. *Man* (N.S.) 8:100–107.
Dominguez, Virginia
    1994   A Taste for "the Other." *Current Anthropology* 35(4):333–338.
Douglas, Mary
    1970   *Natural Symbols: Explorations in Cosmology.* New York: Pantheon
            Books.
Doyle, Kathleen
    1989   Madam C.J. Walker: First Black Woman Millionaire. *American History*
            Illustrated 24(March):24–25.
Drachler, Jacob
    1975   *Black Homeland, Black Diaspora: Cross-Currents of the African*
            Relationship. Port Washington, New York: Kennikat Press.
Drake, St.Clair, and Horace Cayton
    1962   The Measure of a Man. *Black Metropolis: A Study of Negro Life in a*
            Northern City. Vol. 2. New York: Harper, 495–525.
Du Bois, W. E. B.
    1916   That Capital "N." *Crisis* 35(March):184.
    1920   In Black. *Crisis* 20(October):263, 264.
    1928   The Name Negro. *Crisis* 35(March):96–97.
    1933   On Being Ashamed of Oneself. *Crisis* 40(September):199–200.
Dunkling, Leslie, and William Gosling
    1983   *The Facts on File Dictionary of First Names.* New York: Facts on File.
Eagleston, Oran, and Antoinette Clifford
    1945   A Comparative Study of the Names of White and Negro College Students.
            Journal of Social Psychology 21:57–64.
Early, Gerald
    1992   Black Like ... Shirley Temple? *Harpers,* 284(February):33–34.
Ebony Magazine
    1953   America's Ten Best-Dressed Negro Women: Fashion Group Selects Its First
            List in Nation-Wide Poll 8(7):32–35.
    1954   Are Mulattoes Ruling the Race? 9(October):62–63.
    1955   Negro Blue Bloods 10(September):55.
El-Amin, Mustafa
    1991   *The Religion of Islam and the Nation of Islam: What Is the Difference?*
            Newark, New Jersey: El-Amin Publications.
Elliot, H. F. I.
    1948   *The Coiffure of the Masai Warrior.* In Tanganyika Notes and Records.
Elliott, R. S.
    1901   The Story of Our Magazine. *The Colored American Magazine*
            3–4:43–77.
Esedebe, P. Olisanwuche
    1982   *Pan-Africanism: The Idea and Movement.* Washington, D. C.: Howard
            University Press.

Essence
   1996   Advertisement for Accenting High Lighting Duo by Loreal. (April):25.
Everett, Donald
   1952   *Free Persons of Color in New Orleans, 1803–1865.* Ph.D. Dissertation,
           Tulane University.
Fairchild, Halford
   1985   Black, Negro, or Afro-American? The Differences Are Crucial. *Journal of
           Black Studies* 16(1):47–55.
Fanon, Frantz
   1967   *Toward the African Revolution.* New York: Grove Press.
   1968   *Wretched of the Earth.* New York: Grove Press.
Fatton, Robert Jr.
   1997   The Rise, Fall, and Resurrection of President Aristide. In *Haiti Renewed.
           Political and Economic Prospects.* Robert Rotberg (ed.). Washington, D.C.:
           Brookings Institution Press, 136–153.
Ferkiss, Victor
   1966   *Africa's Search for Identity.* New York: George Braziller.
Ferrell, Pamela
   1993   *Where Beauty Touches Me.* Washington, D.C.: Cornrows & Company.
Ferris, William
   1913   *The African Abroad.* New Haven, Conn.: The Tuttle, Morehouse and Tay-
           lor Press.
Fishel, Leslie Jr.
   1980   The 1880s: Pivotal Decade for the Black Community. *Hayes Historical
           Journal* 3:85–94.
Fitchett, E. Horace
   1940   The Traditions of the Free Negro in Charleston, South Carolina. *The
           Journal of Negro History* 25(2):139–152.
Fitzpatrick, Joseph
   1971   The Problem of Color. In *Puerto Rican Americans: The Meaning of
           Migration of the Mainland.* Englewood Cliffs: Prentice-Hall, Inc.
Foner, Eric
   1996   *Freedom's Lawmakers, A Directory of Black Officeholders during
           Reconstruction.* Baton Rouge: Louisiana State University Press.
Fortune, Thomas
   1906   Who Are We? Afro-Americans, Colored People, or Negroes? *Voice of the
           Negro* 3 (March):194–198.
Franklin, John Hope
   1994   *From Slavery to Freedom: A History of African Americans.* New York:
           Alfred A. Knopf.
Frazier, E. Franklin
   1963   *The Negro Church in America.* New York: Schocken Books.
   1966   *The Negro in the United States.* Chicago: University of Chicago Press.
Friedman, Walter
   1996   Malone, Annie Turnbo. *Encyclopedia of Black America.* W. Augustus Low
           and Virgil A. Clift (eds.). New York: McGraw-Hill Book Company.
Fyfe, Christopher
   1962   *History of Sierra Leone.* London: Collier Books.

Gardell, Mattias
  1996   *In the Name of Elijah Muhammad: Louis Farrakhan and the Nation of Islam*. Durham: Duke University Press.
Garvey, Amy Jacques
  1969   *Philosophy and Opinions of Marcus Garvey*. New York: Atheneum.
  1978   *Garvey and Garveyism*. New York: Octagon Books.
Gatewood, Willard
  1990   *Aristocrats of Color: The Black Elite, 1880–1920*. Bloomington: University of Indiana Press.
  1996   Skin Color. *Encyclopedia of African–American Culture and History*. Jack Salzman, David Smith, and Cornel West (eds.). New York: Simon and Schuster.
Gayarré, Charles
  1879   *History of Louisiana*. Vols. 1–4. New Orleans: James A. Gresham.
Gerber, David
  1976   *Black Ohio and the Color Line, 1860–1915*. Urbana: University of Illinois Press.
Gettone, V.
  1981   Negative Label. *Association of Black Psychologists' Newsletter* 12(2):3, 11.
Gibson, Aliona
  1995   *Nappy: Growing Up Black and Female in America*. New York: Harlem River Press.
Goggin, Jacqueline
  1993   Booker T. Washington. In *Black Women in America: An Historical Encyclopedia*. Darlene Hine (ed.). New York: Carlson Publishing, 1226–1228.
Golden, Marita
  1983   *Migrations of the Heart*. Garden City, New York: Ballantine Books.
Goodman, Mary Ellen
  1964   *Race Awareness in Young Children*. New York: Collier Books.
Gossett, T. F.
  1963   *Race: The History of an Idea in America*. Dallas: Southern Methodist University Press.
Graham, Lawrence
  2000   *Our Kind of People: Inside America's Black Upper Class*. New York: HarperCollins.
Grant, George S.
  1926   What Are We? *The Messenger* 8(October):300.
Green, Kim
  1993   The Pain of Living the Lye. *Essence* (June):38.
Greene, Beverly
  1992   Still Here: A Perspective on Psychotherapy with African-American Women. In *New Directions in Feminist Psychology: Practice, Theory, and Research*. J. Chrisler and D. Howard (eds.). New York: Springer, 13–25.
  1993a Psychotherapy with African-American Women: Integrating Feminist and Psychodynamic Models. *Journal of Training and Practice in Professional Psychology* 7(Spring):49–66.

1993b Stereotypes of African-American Sexuality: A Commentary. In *Human Sexuality*. S. Rathus, J. Nevi, and L. Rathus-Fichner (eds.). Boston: Allyn and Bacon.

1994 African American Women. In *Women of Color: Integrating Ethnic and Gender Identities in Psychotherapy*. Lillian Comas-Diaz, and Beverly Greene (eds.). New York: Guilford Press, 10–29.

Hacker, Andrew
1992 *Two Nations: Black and White, Separate, Hostile, Unequal*. New York: Scribner's.

Hackley, Azalia
1916 *The Colored Girl Beautiful*. Kansas City: Burton Publishing Company.

Hall, Ronald
1995 The Bleaching Syndrome: African Americans' Response to Cultural Domination vis-a-vis Skin Color. *Journal of Black Studies* 26(2):172–184.

Hall, Stuart
1991 Signification, Representation, Ideology: Althusser and the Post-Structuralist Debates. In *Critical Perspectives on Media and Society*. Robert K. Avery and David Eason (eds.). New York: The Guilford Press, 88–113.

Hallpike, Christopher Robert
1969 Social Hair. *Man* (N.S.) 4:254–98.

1988 New Ethnicities. *ICA Document 7*. London: ICA. 27–31.

Hamilton, Kendra
2001 Embracing 'Black Is Beautiful.' *Black Issues in Higher Education* 17(23):34.

Hardy, James
1995 The River of De-Nile. *The Advocate* 697(26 December).

Harley, Sharon
1996 *The Timetables of African—American History. A Chronology of the Most Important People and Events in African–American History*. New York: Simon and Schuster.

Harris, Joseph
1971 *The African Presence in Asia: Consequences of the East African Slave Trade*. Evanston, Illinois: Northwestern University Press.

1974 *East African Slave Trade and Repatriation to Kenya*. Washington, D. C.: Howard University.

Harris, Marvin
1968 *The Rise of Anthropological Theory: A History of Theories of Culture*. New York: Thomas Y. Crowell.

Harris, Peter
1991 Bonding by Braiding. *Essence* 21(March):25.

Harris, Robert
1981 Charleston's Free Afro-American Elite: The Brown Fellowship Society. *South Carolina Historical Magazine* 72:289–310.

Henry, Howell
1914 *The Police Control of the Slave in South Carolina*. Ph.D. Dissertation. Emory, Virginia, Vanderbilt University.

Hernton, Calvin
  1965   *Sex and Racism in America*. New York: Grove.
Herron, Carolivia
  1997   *Nappy Hair*. New York: Alfred A. Knopf.
Hershman, P.
  1974   Hair, Sex, and Dirt. *Man* (N.S.) 9:274–98.
Hine, Darlene
  1993   *Black Women in America: An Historical Encyclopedia*. Brooklyn, New
          York: Carlson Publishing.
Hirsch, Arnold, and Joseph Logsdon, eds.
  1992   *Creole New Orleans: Race and Americanization*. Baton Rouge: Louisiana
          State University Press.
Holloway Scrapbook
Holt, Thomas
  1977   *Black Over White: Negro Political Leadership in South Carolina During
          Reconstruction*. Urbana: University of Illinois Press.
hooks, bell
  1993   *Sisters of the Yam: Black Women and Self-Recovery*. Boston: South End
          Press.
  1995   *Killing Rage. Ending Racism*. New York: Henry Holt and Company.
Hopkins, Tracy
  1995   The Darker the Berry. In *Testimony: Young African-Americans on
          Self-Discovery and Black Identity*. Natasha Tarpley (ed.). Boston: Beacon
          Press, 231–235.
Horton, James
  1993   *Free People of Color: Inside the African American Community*. Washing-
          ton, D.C.: Smithsonian Institution Press.
Hughes, Langston
  1979   (1934) *The Ways of White Folks*. New York: Alfred A. Knopf.
Isaacs, Harold
  1964   *The New World of Negro Americans*. London: Phoenix House.
Jackson, Luther
  1968   *Free Negro Labor and Property Holding in Virginia*. New York: Atheneum.
Jenkins, Edward
  1996   *To Fathom More: African American Scientists and Inventors*.
          Latham: University Press of America.
Jet Magazine
  1986   AHBAI Demands Apology for Revlon Racial Slur. Vol. 71(October):14.
Johnson, Michael, and James Roark
  1982   "A Middle Ground": Free Mulattos and the Friendly Moralist
          Society of Antebellum Charleston. *Southern Studies* 21(3):246–265.
Jones, Beverly
  1990   Quest of Equality: The Life and Writings of Mary Eliza Church Terrell,
          1863–1954. In *Black Women in United States History*. Darlene Clark Hine
          (ed.). New York: Carlson Publishing.
Jones, Lisa
  1994   The Hair Trade. In *Bulletproof Diva: Tales of Race, Sex, and Hair*. New
          York: Doubleday, 278–297.

Jones, Norrece Jr.
    1990   *Born a Child of Freedom, Yet a Slave: Mechanisms of Control and Strate-
            gies of Resistance in Antebellum South Carolina.* Hanover: Wesleyan
            University Press.
Jordan, W. D.
    1968   *White over Black: American Attitudes Toward the Negro, 1500–1812.*
            Chapel Hill: University of North Carolina Press.
Katz, Daniel, and Kenneth Braly
    1935–1936   Racial Prejudice and Racial Stereotypes. *The Journal of Abnormal
                and Social Psychology* 30:175–193.
Kaye, Melanie Kantrowitz
    1996   Jews in the U.S.: The Rising Costs of Whiteness. In *Names We Call Home.*
            Becky Thompson and Sangeeta Tyagi (eds.). London: Routledge,
            121–137.
Keith, Verna, and Cedric Herring
    1991   Skin Tone Stratification in the Black Community. *American Journal of
            Sociology* 97(November):760–78.
Kenyatta, Kamau, and Janice Kenyatta
    1996   *Black Folk's Hair, Secrets, Shame and Liberation.* Somerset, New Jersey:
            Songhai Publication.
Kinard, Tulani
    1997   *No Lye!* New York: St. Martin's Griffin.
Kitwana, Bakari
    1995   *The Rap on Gangsta Rap. Who Run It? Gangsta Rap and Visions of Black
            Violence.* Chicago: Third World Press.
Kly, Y. N.
    1985   *International Law and the Black Minority in the United States.* School of
            Human Justice: University of Regina, Canada.
Koger, Larry
    1985   *Black Slave Owners: Free Black Slave Masters in South Carolina,
            1790–1860.* Jefferson, North Carolina: McFarland.
Kolchin, Peter
    1993   *American Slavery, 1619–1877.* New York: Hill and Wang.
Krapp, Kristine
    1999   *Notable Black Americans.* Detroit: Gale Group.
Lake, Obiagele
    1993   Cultural Beliefs and Breast Feeding Practices Among Jamaican Rastafari-
            ans. *Cajanus* 25(4):201–214.
    1994   The Many Voices of Rastafarian Women. *New West Indian Guide*
            68(3&4):135–157.
    1995   Toward a Pan-African Identity: Diaspora African Repatriates in Ghana.
            Anthropological Quarterly 68(1):21–36.
    1998   *RastafarI Women. Subordination in the Midst of Liberation Theology.*
            Durham: Carolina Academic Press.
Lanker, Brian
    1989   *I Dream A World: Portraits of Black Women Who Changed America.*
            New York: Stewart, Tabori & Chang.

Lasker, G. W.
    1980   Surnames in the Study of Human Biology. *American Anthropologist*
            82(3):525–538.
Leach, Edmund R.
    1958   Magical Hair. *Journal of the Royal Anthropological Institute* 88:147–64.
Lerner, Gerda
    1972   *Black Women in White America.* New York: Vintage.
Lessing, E. E., and S. W. Zagorin
    1972   Black Power Ideology and College Students' Attitudes toward Their Own
            and Other Racial Groups. *Journal of Personality and Social Psychology*
            21:61–73.
Lewis, Rupert
    1988   *Marcus Garvey: Anti-Colonial Champion.* Trenton: Africa World Press.
Liebenow, J. Gus
    1969   *Liberia. The Evolution of Privilege.* Ithaca, N.Y.: Cornell University Press.
Littlefield, Daniel Jr., and Lonnie Underhill
    1971   Renaming the American Indian, 1890–1913. *American Studies* 12(2):33–45.
Llorens, David
    1967   Natural Hair, New Symbol of Race Pride. *Ebony* 23 (December):
            139–144.
Lockhart, James
    1992   *The Nahuas After the Conquest: A Social and Cultural History of the
            Indians of Central Mexico, Sixteenth through Eighteenth Centuries.*
            Stanford: Stanford University Press.
Lommel, Cookie
    1993   *Madam C. J. Walker, Entrepreneur.* Los Angeles: Melrose Square.
Longshore, D.
    1979   Color Connotations and Racial Attitudes. *Journal of Black Studies*
            10(2):183–197.
Longshore, D., and R. Beilin
    1980   Interracial Behavior in the Prisoner's Dilemma: The Effect of Color
            Connotations. *Journal of Black Studies* 11(1):105–120.
Lorde, Audre
    1986   *Our Dead Behind Us.* New York: W. W. Norton, 62.
    1990   Is Your Hair Still Political? *Essence* 21 (September):40.
Lutz, Catherine
    1973   Ethnicity: Strategies of Collective and Individual Impression Management.
            Social Research 40:344–65.
Madhubuti, Haki
    1994   Language: Is There a Black Way? In *Claiming Earth: Race, Rage, Rape,
            Redemption; Blacks Seeking a Culture of Enlightened Empowerment.*
            Chicago: Third World Press.
Mageo, Jeannette Marie
    1994   Hairdo and Don'ts: Hair Symbolism and Sexual History in Samoa. *Man*
            29:407–432.
Malik-Khatib, Syed
    1995   Personal Names and Name Changes. *Journal of Black Studies*
            25(3):349–353.

Marable, Manning
   1991   *Race, Reform, and Rebellion: The Second Reconstruction in Black America, 1945–1990.* Jackson: University Press of Mississippi.
Marsh, Clifton
   1984   *From Black Muslims to Muslims: The Transition from Separatism to Islam, 1930–1980.* London: Scarecrow Press.
Martin, Tony
   1976   *Race First: Ideology and Organizational Struggles of Marcus Garvey and the Universal Negro Improvement Association.* Westport: Greenwood Press.
Mazrui, Ali
   1986   Africa's Identity: The Western Aftermath. In *The Africans: A Triple Heritage.* Boston: Little, Brown, pp. 99–113.
McAdoo, Harriette Pipes
   1980   *Black Families.* Beverly Hills: Sage.
Mercer, Kobena
   1994   In *Welcome to the Jungle.* New York: Routledge, 97–130.
The Messenger
   1924   Society Leaders of Richmond, Va. (May) 6(5), p. 152.
Miller, Floyd J.
   1975   *The Search for a Black Nationality: Black Emigration and Colonization, 1787–1863.* Chicago: University of Illinois Press.
Miller, Kelly
   1925   These "Colored" United States: South Carolina, *The Messenger* 7(11):376, 391, 400.
Mirande, Alfredo
   1985   *The Chicano Experience: An Alternative Perspective.* Notre Dame, Indiana: University of Notre Dame Press.
Moore, Jacquiline
   1994   *A Drop of African Blood: The Washington Black Elite from 1880 to 1920.* Doctoral Dissertation. Department of History, University of Maryland.
Moore, Richard B.
   1960   *The Name "Negro," Its Origin and Evil Use.* New York: Afro-American Publishers.
Morrison, Toni
   1970   *The Bluest Eye.* New York: Washington Square Press.
Morrow, Willie
   1973   *400 Years Without a Comb.* Black Publishers of San Diego.
Moses, Wilson J.
   1978   *The Golden Age of Black Nationalism: 1850–1925.* Hamden, Conn.: Archon Books.
Neal, A.
   1988   The Influence of Skin Color and Facial Features on Perceptions of Black Female Physical Attractiveness. Unpublished Doctoral Dissertation, DePaul University, Chicago.
Neal, A., and M. Wilson
   1989   The Role of Skin Color and Features in the Black Community: Implications for Black Women and Therapy. *Clinical Psychology Review* 9:323–333.

Nelson, Jill
   1990   Mo Better Spike. *Essence* 21 (August):55.
Nettleford, Rex
   1973   National Identity and Attitudes to Race in Jamaica. In *Consequences
          of Class and Color: West Indian Perspectives*. Garden City: Anchor
          Press.
New York Times
   1905   Didn't Make Negroes White. Fake Lotion Concerns Barred from the Use of
          the Mails. 19 (June):12.
Obadeli, Imari
   1972   The Struggle Is for Land. *The Black Scholar* 3(6):24–35.
   1986   *A Macro Level Theory of Human Organization*. Washington: Song of
          Songhay.
Okazawa-Rey, M., T. Robinson, and J. V. Ward
   1987   Black Women and the Politics of Skin Color and Hair. *Women and
          Therapy* 6:89–102.
Ottley, Roi
   1968   *New World A-Coming?* New York: Arno Press.
Painter, Nell
   1996   *Sojourner Truth: A Life, A Symbol*. New York: Norton and Company.
Patterson, Orlando
   1982   *Slavery and Social Death*. Cambridge: Harvard University Press.
Paustian, P. Robert
   1978   The Evolution of Naming Practices among American Blacks. *Names*
          26:177–191.
Pharr, Pauline
   1993   Onomastic Divergence: A Study of Given-Name Trends Among African
          Americans. *American Speech* 68(4):400–409.
Phillips, William Jr.
   1985   *Slavery from Roman Times to the Early Transatlantic Trade*. Minneapolis:
          University of Minnesota Press.
Pierson, Donald
   1942   *Negroes in Brazil. A Study of Race Contact in Bahia*. Chicago:
          University of Chicago Press.
Pinkney, Alphonso
   1984   *The Myth of Black Progress*. London: Cambridge University Press.
Powers, Bernard Jr.
   1994   *Black Charlestonians: A Social History, 1822–1885*. Fayetteville:
          University of Arkansas Press.
Prucha, Paul F.
   1984   *The Great Father: The United States Government and the American
          Indians*. Vol. 2. Lincoln: University of Nebraska Press.
Puckett, Newbell
   1975   *Black Names in America: Origins and Usage*. Murray Heller (ed.). Boston:
          Hall.
Rabinowitz, Howard H.
   1978   *Race Relations in the Urban South, 1865–1890*. New York: Oxford
          University Press.

Redkey, Edwin S.
    1969   *Black Exodus. Black Nationalist and Back to Africa Movements,*
            1890–1910. New Haven: Yale University Press.
Reuter, Edward
    1918   *The Mulatto in the United States.* Boston: Richard G. Badger.
Rigsby, Gregory U.
    1987   *Alexander Crummel: Pioneer in Nineteenth-Century Pan-African*
            Thought. Westport, Conn.: Greenwood Press.
Riley, Denise
    1988   *"Am I That Name?" Feminism and the Category of "Women"*
            in History. Minneapolis: University of Minnesota Press.
Robbins, Faye Wellborn
    1980   *A World-within-a-World: Black Nashville, 1880–1915.* Doctoral
            Dissertation. University of Arkansas.
Robinson, Randall
    2000   *The Debt: What America Owes to Blacks.* New York: Plume.
Rogers, Joel
    1926   What Are We, Negroes or Americans? *The Messenger* 8:237–
            38, 255.
Rogers vs. American Airlines
    1981   527 F. Supp. 229 (S.D.N.Y. 1981).
Rooks, Noliwe
    1996   *Hair Raising: Beauty, Culture, and African American Women.* New Jer-
            sey: Rutgers University Press.
Ross, Kimberly
    1995   Interview Data from Research Project on Attitudes about Straightened and
            Natural Hair. Department of Anthropology, University of Iowa. Iowa City,
            Iowa.
Rules of Regulations, Brown Fellowship Society
    1790   Charleston, South Carolina.
Rules and Regulations of the Friendly Moralist Society
    1848   Charleston, South Carolina.
Rushing, Andrea Benton
    1988   Hair-Raising. *Feminist Studies* 14(2):325–335.
Russell, Kathy, Midge Wilson, and Ronald Hall
    1992   *The Color Complex: The Politics of Skin Color Among African Americans.*
            New York: Harcourt Brace Jovanovich.
Safran, William
    1991   Diasporas in Modern Societies: Myths of Homeland and Return. *Diaspora*
            1(1):83–89.
Sagay, Esi
    1983   *African Hairstyles: Styles of Yesterday and Today.* Portsmouth, N. H.:
            Heinemann.
Sandler, Kathe
    1992   *A Question of Color.* Videorecording. Film Two Productions.
Sayers, Sophia
    1995   To Weave or Not to Weave. *Essence* 26(October):162.

Schapera, Isaac
   1930   *The Khoisan Peoples of South Africa: Bushmen and Hottentots.* London:
          G. Routledge and Sons.
Scherz, Anneliese, E.R. Scherz, G. Taapopi, and A. Otto
   1992   *Hair-Styles, Head-dresses and Ornaments.* Windhoek, Namibia:
          Gamsberg Macmillan Publishers.
Schweninger, Loren
   1990   *Black Property Owners in the South—1790–1915.* Chicago: University of
          Illinois Press.
Scott, Joan
   1992   Multiculturalism and the Politics of Identity. *October* 61:12–19.
Shick, Tom
   1980   *Behold the Promised Land. A History of Afro-American Settler Society in
          Nineteenth Century Liberia.* Baltimore: John Hopkins University Press.
Sisters in Style
   1996   Max advertisement. 25.
Skinner, Elliott P., and Pearl Robinson
   1983   Afro-Americans in Search of Africa: The Scholar's Dilemma. In *Transition
          and Resiliency in Africa.* Washington, D. C.: Howard University Press, pp.
          3–26.
Smith, Jessie Carney, ed.
   1992   Nannie Helen Burroughs. *Notable Black American Women.* Detroit: Gale
          Research, 1886.
   1996   *Notable Black American Women.* Volume Two. New York: Gale Research.
Sonuga, 'Kunle
   1976   *Traditional Hairstyles for the Blackwoman.* Bell Publicity.
Stanton, Elizabeth Cady, Susan B. Anthony, and Matilda Joslyn Gage
   1883   *History of Woman Suffrage.* Vol. 3. New York: Fowler and Wells.
Steele, Shelby
   1990   *The Content of Our Character: A New Vision of Race in America.*
          New York: St. Martin's Press.
Sterling, Dorothy
   1984   *We Are Your Sisters: Black Women in the Nineteenth Century.* New York:
          W. W. Norton.
Sterling, Dorothy
   1988   *Black Foremothers: Three Lives.* New York: The Feminist Press.
Stevenson, Michael
   1991–1992   Total War: Europeans and Indigenous Peoples in the Columbia
               Epoch. *Anthropological Forum* 6(3):321–337.
Streitmatter, Roger
   1994   *Raising Her Voice: African American Women Journalists Who Changed
          History.* Lexington, Kentucky: University of Kentucky Press.
Strutton, David, and James Lumpkin
   1993   Stereotypes of Black In-Group Attractiveness in Advertising: On Possible
          Psychological Effects. *Psychological Reports* 73:507–511.
Stuckey, Sterling
   1987   *Slave Culture: Nationalist Theory and the Foundation of Black America.*
          New York: Oxford University Press.

Stutzman, R.
    1981   El Mestizaje: An All-Inclusive Ideology of Exclusion. In *Cultural Transfor-*
           mations and Ethnicity in Modern Ecuador. N. E. Whitten, Jr. (ed.). New
           York: Harper and Row, 45–93.
Tarpley, Natasha
    1995   *Testimony: Young African-Americans on Self-Discovery and Black Iden-*
           tity. Boston: Beacon Press.
Thompson, Cliff
    1995   Inventing Our Names, Our Selves. *Commonweal* 222(6):30.
Thornton, John
    1992   *Africa and Africans in the Making of the Atlantic World 1400–1680.*
           Cambridge: Cambridge University Press, 230.
Toll, William
    1979   *The Resurgence of Race. Black Social Theory from Reconstruction to the*
           Pan-African Conferences. Philadelphia, Temple University Press.
           The Relevance of the People's Revolutionary Party to Africans World-
           Wide. Mimeograph No. 3. The All-African People's Revolutionary Party.
Tourgée, Albion
    1890   *Pactolus Prime.* New York: Irvington Publishers.
Ture, Kwame
    n.d.
Turner, Edward
    1911   *Slavery in Pennsylvania.* Ph.D. Dissertation, Johns Hopkins University.
Turner, Jonathan, Royce Singleton Jr., and David Musick
    1984   *Oppression: A Social-History of Black-White Relations in America.*
           Chicago: Nelson-Hall.
Turner, Martha Anne
    1971   *The Yellow Rose of Texas: The Story of a Song.* El Paso: University of
           Texas.
    1976   *The Yellow Rose of Texas: Her Saga and Her Song.* Austin, Texas: Shoal
           Creek.
United States Reports. Cases Adjudged in the Supreme Court.
    1916   Plessy vs. Ferguson, pp. 538–564. New York: The Banks Law Publishing
           Company.
Uya, Okon
    1971   *Black Brotherhood: Afro-Americans and Africa.* Lexington, Mass.: D. C. Heath.
Van Deburg, William
    1992   *New Day in Babylon. The Black Power Movement and American Culture,*
           1965–1975. Chicago: University of Chicago Press.
Walker, Alice
    1983   If the Present Looks Like the Past, What Does the Future Look Like? In *In*
           Search of Our Mother's Gardens. San Diego: Harcourt, 290–312.
    1984   Without Commercials. In *Horses Make the Landscape Look More Beauti-*
           ful. San Diego: Harcourt Brace Jovanovich, 55–58.
Walker, Sheila
    1977   What's in a Name? *Ebony* 32(8):74–76.
Wallace, Michele
    1979   *Black Macho and the Myth of the Superwoman.* New York: Dial.

Wang, Penelope, and Maggie Malone
    1986   Targeting Black Dollars. *Newsweek* 108 (October):54–55.
Washington, Elsie
    1988   The Bluest Eye? *Essence* 18(January):114.
Washington, Jesse
    1995   A Lighter Shade of Black. *Essence* 25(January):40.
The Washington Bee
    1909   White Men in Louisiana Marrying Colored Women. (Oct. 23):21.
    1910   Would You Like Your Face Lighter Colored for Every Important
               Occasion? 30(29 Jan):38.
    1910   Straighten the Hair. (Mar. 5):43.
Waters, Anita M.
    1985   *Race, Class, and Political Symbols: Rastafari and Jamaican Politics.*
               New Brunswick: Transaction Books.
Webber, Thomas L.
    1978   *Deep Like the Rivers, Education in the Slave Quarter Community,*
               1831–1865. New York: W. W. Norton.
Webster, Raymond
    1999   *African American Firsts in Science and Technology.* Detroit: Gale
               Group.
Webster, Yehudi O.
    1992   *The Racialization of America.* New York: St. Martin's Press.
Weisbord, Robert
    1969   Africa, Africans and the Afro-American: Images and Identities in Transi-
               tion. *Race* 10(January):305–321.
    1973   *Ebony Kinship. Africa, Africans, and the Afro-American.* Westport,
               Conn.: Greenwood Press.
Wells-Barnett, Ida B.
    1970   *Crusade for Justice: The Autobiography of Ida B. Wells.* Alfreda M. Duster
               (ed.). Chicago: University of Chicago Press.
White, Deborah
    1985   *Ar'n't I a Woman: Female Slaves in the Plantation South.* New York:
               W. W. Norton.
White, Shane, and Graham White
    1995   Slave Hair and African American Culture in the Eighteenth and
               Nineteenth Centuries. *The Journal of Southern History.*
               41(February):45–76.
Wikramanayake, Marina
    1966   *The Free Negro in Ante-Bellum South Carolina.* Doctoral Dissertation,
               University of Wisconsin.
    1973   *A World in Shadow: The Free Black in Antebellum South Carolina.*
               Columbia, S. C.: University of South Carolina Press.
Wilkerson, Isabel
    1989   Many Who Are Black Favor New Term for Who They Are. *New York
               Times* 1(January 31):14.
Wilkinson, Doris
    1990   Americans of African Identity. *Society* 27(4):14–18.

Williams, John, Richard Tucker, and Frances Dunham
    1971   Changes in the Connotations of Color Names Among Negroes and
            Caucasians: 1963–1969. *Journal of Personality and Social Psychology*
            19:222–228.
Williams, Oscar, ed.
    1969   Afro-American vs. Negro: A 19th-Century Essay Against the Use of the
            Term "Negro." *Negro History Bulletin* 32(March):18.
Williamson, Joel
    1980   *New People: Miscegenation and Mulattoes in the United States*. New
            York: Free Press.
Williamson, Mark Herbert
    1979   Powhatan Hair. *Man* (N.S.) 14:392–413.
Wilson, Calvin
    1912   Negroes Who Owned Slaves. *Popular Science Monthly* 81:483–494.
Wilson, William J.
    1978   *The Declining Significance of Race*. Chicago: University of Chicago Press.
Wood, Peter
    1974   *Black Majority: Negroes in Colonial South Carolina From 1670 through
            the Stono Rebellion*. New York: Alfred A. Knopf.
Woodson, Carter
    1924   Free Negro Owners of Slaves in the United States in 1830. *Journal of
            Negro History* 9(January):41–85.
    1990   *The Miseducation of the Negro*. Trenton, N.J.: Africa World Press.
Yellin, Jean
    1989   *Women and Sisters: The Anti-Slavery Feminists in American Culture*.
            New Haven: Yale University Press.
Zinn, Maxine, and Bonnie Dill
    1994   *Women of Color in U. S. Society*. Philadelphia: Temple University Press.

Name Index

Subject Index

About the Author

OBIAGELE LAKE is an independent scholar in Kansas City, Missouri.